A MANAGER'S GUIDE TO THE MILLENNIUM

A MANAGER'S GUIDE TO THE MILLENNIUM

Today's Strategies for Tomorrow's Success

Ken Matejka
Richard J. Dunsing

amacom

American Management Association

New York · Atlanta · Boston · Chicago · Kansas City · San Francisco · Washington, D. C.
Brussels · Mexico City · Tokyo · Toronto

Library of Congress Cataloging-in-Publication Data

Matejka, Kén
    A manager's guide to the millennium: today's strategies for
tomorrow's success
    Matejka, Richard J. Dunsing.
        p.   cm.
    Includes bibliographical references and index.
    ISBN 0-8144-0269-0
    1. Management.   I. Dunsing, Richard J.   II. Title.   III. Title:
Faith, hope, and clarity.
    HD31.M3373   1995
    658—dc20   94-47650
                                                        CIP

Printing number

10   9   8   7   6   5   4   3   2

Ken Matejka: To my wife, Sally Carmichael Matejka—thanks for your love, support, help, and the lost family time caused by the writing of this book. To my daughter, Anastasia Louise Matejka—thanks for your love, passion, and creative ideas. To my parents, Mary and Joseph Matejka—thanks for your love and sacrifices.

Richard J. Dunsing: To my wife, Carol Jean Dunsing, who always inspired me to see the best in people and to see the bigger picture. To my children, Steve, Susan, Sharon, and Sandi, who bring their enthusiasm for life into their work, and who are in the grand flow of problems and possibilities within organizations in the coming era. It is for their generation, and the two generations that bracket them, that this book is meant to be a guide.

Contents

A Parable

Dream Together, Drawn Together

In the beginning, there were only a few, and they were drawn together in dreaming. The seed was a vision, a grand scheme, a quest. And it was so very good. Although small in number, they were strong, these dreamers, and they shared that vision and worked toward it in great concert. And their good work spun off minidreams and subdreams and branch dreams. Quickly, the dream-task needed many more dream-seekers, and so the number of people clustered around the dream grew greatly. Some noticed, but others did not, that something called *organization* was happening to them. It was unexpected, for the dream made no mention of organization, and so the dreamers searched all the land for a map or blueprint. Strangely, they found none. It seemed that dreams were the most shapeless of things and, perhaps with very good reason, left no clues to organization.

The dreamers then observed other clusters of people gathered around a dream. When they looked, they saw row upon row of pyramids. Not knowing any better (or worse, really), they formed their own pyramid.

Time passed in this place of slots and levels. The people near the top of the pyramid continued to talk about their dream. They also spent a lot of time shouting encouragement to those further down the pyramid. But continuing to dream became more difficult, since the pyramid itself seemed to require more and more maintenance. Of course, people in other pyramids were curious about what they were up to, so they often had to spend time talking to those people about their pyramid. Such encroaching business soon almost completely distracted them from doing more creative dreaming.

Along the foundation of the pyramid, of course, were many people who were acting on the many possible applications of the dream. They generated many needs and wants as they responded to the calls of encouragement from above. It's not that they were ungrateful for encouraging words, but they did seek tangible support from those above them. They wanted information, resources of every sort with which to better carry out the dream, and they wanted to know more about the dream and what was happening to it. They hoped that their efforts were helping to keep the dream alive.

Later, and much too late, someone who nobody could afford to ignore lamented the new widespread lack of respect for the dream. "Something should be done." The person who sat at the peak of the pyramid once again spoke to all within the pyramid about the dream. The speech rang forth. It tingled many spines. But it also confused many people. The dream seemed tattered, vague, murky, and even a little hokey. In the silence that followed, an electric truth swept the pyramid, and in one indignant voice the people said, "Why, we have already done that. Where have you been? What have you been doing?" The original dream had long since been given life. Its cycle was over, but no new dream had taken its place.

New speeches were hastily prepared. These speeches deplored the dreamless state of affairs. Task forces were formed to get to the bottom of this dreadful situation. Dreams were quickly invented and just as quickly abandoned. Attempts to buy or lease someone else's dream worked not at all. Months later, the people were as dreamless as ever. The truth quietly settled like dust within the pyramid. There was now no real place or space for dream making, only dream chasing.

For many people, that mattered not. Chasing was more

than good enough. Others were simply content to follow the myth or history of the old dream. At least being dreamless explained many odd happenings.

And so it was that this pyramid had attracted many good and able people, for in this place, all were treated well and fairly. It was to be expected, not surprisingly, that they would apply themselves with great vigor and stoke up great cauldrons of energy. But without an exciting core dream, they seldom knew where or how to connect their mighty force of energy. Some invented dreams of their own. Others spent themselves working on the pyramid and creating sub-pyramids to overcome the dreamless state with efficiency. Some invented personal dreams and worked on those while pretending to be working on the original dream. Surely, too, they spent much time complaining, blaming, and fearing.

Other things changed, too. While they were busy struggling for their new dream, other organizations everywhere were engaging dreams of their own. And those dreams generated brand-new forms, unrecognizable as pyramids. In fact, organizations took many new forms, including collages, prisms, and a collection of free-floating particles.

Good people though they are, the fate of those within the pyramid is still in doubt. Powerful dreams need fertile soil, a conducive climate, and careful tending. There are also many dream diseases that can kill the dream in the becoming. Leaving the dreaming to the official dreaming departments is one way to proceed. Specialists build brittle dreams with sharp, jagged edges. But many people just can't wear designer dreams. Dreaming in numbers (numerical dreaming) is another fatal disease, for such dreamers think in long division, not long vision. When in doubt, they typically add many new bored members. And, of course, being driven by nightmares (which are very different things from dreams) is a sure way to stunt the possibilities of the pyramid.

Alas, this story of dreams ends for now. The people in the pyramid built around a long-gone dream will probably survive. It is only just that they should. But if they cannot find a way to invent a captivating dream soon to serve as the focus of their quest, much will be lost. Without a vivid, valid dream, they will have no focused power, no ecstasy to share, and no celebrations, for without a goal, victory cannot be defined and achieved.

Worst of all, they will have no chance to learn how to dream and dream again . . . for it is the dreaming itself that most beautifully shapes organizations and the people in them.

Acknowledgments

Ken Matejka: My special thanks to Duquesne University for allowing me to take a sabbatical to prepare this book. I am grateful to my colleagues at the A. J. Palumbo School of Business for the support and creative environments that allowed me to learn the necessary insights needed to create and sculpt my contributions to the material in this book. I am indebted to the thousands of executives, managers, leaders, administrators, and students with whom I have had the privilege of collaborating. Through them, I learned the urgently felt need to change organizational life for the better. Finally, a huge thanks to our editor, Adrienne Hickey, for having faith and hope in our clarity.

Richard J. Dunsing: I am grateful for the University of Richmond and the Robins School of Business which continue to nurture an environment for learning about management and organizations. I thank the many organizations and their caring and committed people who joined me in workshops, retreats, and seminars over the years. Learning was always a joint venture, as it must be. They continue the noble task and ongoing struggle to make sense and do well in complex and chaotic times.

And thanks to the Management Institute faculty and staff who follow their mission of learning and teaching how organizations and their people can make a difference. Thanks, too, to Ercelle Ridley for keeping me on track.

I thank, too, mentors, guides, and inspirations: Bob Harper at Knox College, Stan Herman now in California, Tom Reuschling, now in Florida, and Robert James Waller, who once was a mere business school dean.

A
MANAGER'S
GUIDE
TO THE
MILLENNIUM

Introduction

Faith, Hope & Clarity

Parables poke at meanings on different levels. In the parable of the mythical organization, the organization lost its sense of itself over time, and the people saw poorly through a mist of confusing connections, conflicting directions, and external reflections. Perplexed, they benchmarked what others were doing, copied the pyramid style at a time when it was about to fade, and stopped monitoring their environment. Soon, they were lost, and their new, prized pyramid, the only one left, was ironically the engineer of their demise.

From "Maximum Security Cells" to "Minimum Security Prisms"

Welcome to Nomads' Land, where professional tribes with no permanent abode wander from organization to organization. In the past, as we suggested in our opening parable, organizations resembled pyramids (solid, stepped, and sharply sloping to a point) consisting of many levels of "maximum security cells." Each employee had a clearly defined level and cell (work space and job specifications), and, in exchange for good behavior, each received maximum job security.

We think that tomorrow's emerging organizations will be more like "minimum security prisms." "Minimum security" suggests that all guarantees, promises, and loyalty oaths, if not yet canceled, are on short notice. Therefore, all organizational players must see themselves as "temps" (temporaries or nomads). The only permanent occupation for all of us will be getting ready for the "coming battles undefined." In addition, we believe that organizations, like glass prisms, will be solid but transparent, quickly changing the direction and shape of anything passing through them, resisting discipline, and reflecting and refracting light, energy, talent and wisdom into a spectrum of colorful hues. We view these prisms as permeable instruments that will permit the free flow of agents through the organization at any point (like porous rocks or, better yet, flow-through tea bags).

Defining the Challenge

This book is a millennium readiness manual that will help you successfully manage your future in the new minimum security prisms. It is about paradoxes, paradigms, and new possibilities. The material tries to make sense out of changing current and conjectured twenty-first-century management practices and to provide possible response strategies. The good news is that this book is about your success—personal and organizational—today and tomorrow! We invite you to trigger some new thoughts, redesign some old theories, and develop creative perspectives about yourself, your future, and your career and about managing people in the new millennium. The bad news is that this book is also about some potential land mines and swamps—for example, desperately holding onto the past, running mindlessly and faddishly into the future, and counting on any given organization to offer you long-term security.

It's easy to predict the future. It's being right that's hard! Nonetheless, we will make some predictions about the world on the other side of the year 2000 time/mind barrier. Predicting is a minimal science because some shifts will be unexpected, profound, and unprecedented. But any leader in today's climate must be able to detect, understand, and react intelligently to the potential paradigm shifts. We are already on the launch pad of the twenty-first century, and the countdown has begun. You will be both passengers and pilots on the organizational ride into the next millennium. You are the empowered managers, leaders, and professionals who will make it all work.

The starting point for any great journey is shaping the right questions:

- What will this brave new world of work look like?
- What skills will you need to succeed?
- How can you make sense out of the flood of events?
- What forms and kinds of organizations will last?
- What will you do when the organizational cycle ends and your job evaporates?
- Why do good people hopelessly hang onto the past?
- What outdated information contaminates your decision making?
- What environmental changes will force behavioral change?
- What are the differences among fearlessness, avoidance, and denial in facing a bright or dangerous future?
- When is resistance to change your friend, and when is it your enemy?
- Which is more prophetic—"virtual reality" or "virtual ignorance"?
- How can you, the millennium manager, make timely and accurate decisions in the here and now that anticipate and fit the unknowable future?

Identifying Our Potential Readers

This book was written for managers, leaders, and professionals who want to make some sense out of what is happening to management and organizations and who want to work positively with, through, around, and inside these instruments. If you accept the truth that you can't avoid this thing called organization (which will always be there in some way, shape, or form), then knowing how to decipher the configuration is a necessary skill.

Only by implication will the thoughts and views in this book apply to the CEOs of the world's top two thousand companies. Our ideas apply mostly to those who must dance in the CEO's show. This book is for people who want their organization to "be" well (be an honest, ethical, caring place to work) and to "do" well (be effective, competitive, and achieving—all those powerful, get-it-done words). It is for people who want to "serve" in the organization and to be enhanced by that experience.

This book is for people who want to help the organization become an instrument for customer satisfaction—without becoming a casualty in order to make that happen. It is for people who want to give at the office without having to sacrifice their inner spirit as it is and as it might become, given a chance. It is for the managers, leaders, and professionals (often there is no real distinction) who don't want to be never-at-home parents.

The Mission of the Book

For those who choose the millennium organizational voyage, this is a book about *faith, hope,* and *clarity.* Our mission is to encourage you, the organizational traveler:

- To shape the deeper question before you choose the answer
- To assess what is happening around you and to you
- To hear and appreciate your creative internal voices better

We also strive:

- To try to put our own unique spin on the understanding of tomorrow's world of work

- To highlight some dysfunctions that result in humanistically impaired organizations
- To remind you that "under the circumstances" is no place to be

You Are the "People of Promise"

The very fact that you are holding this book, thinking about reading it, makes you one of the "people of promise"! Who are the people of promise? They are the employees who are ambitious, able, at least moderately willing to accept change and ambiguity, and concerned enough to differentiate between truth and fiction—people who really want to make organizations work! Whether you are twenty-five years old and trying to get a handle on behaviors in your shop or fifty-five years old but still interested in trying to help your company stay vibrant, this book will help you to participate more actively and constructively in the organizational world of tomorrow. In an even broader sense, understanding some future possibilities and proactive strategies should be invaluable for advising your children, spouses, or friends about the best way to prepare for tomorrow. "People of promise" aren't naive, but they want to be hopeful and helpful in overcoming skepticism, helplessness, and resentment in organizations. They understand that successful answers are a mix of logic and magic.

How the Book Is Organized

This book is divided into three parts. In Part One, we scope some pertinent future trends and the resulting new behavioral traits needed; uncover paradoxes, paradigms, and new possibilities; and examine the critical issue of how to differentiate among meaningful changes, enduring truths, fallacies and fads. When should change be embraced? When should change be resisted?

In Part Two, we redefine four skills needed to build the Optimum Organization Zone, or "O-Zone": Making the Dream,

Building the Dream Team, Hooking Everyone into the Dream, and Etching the Clarity. The focus of Part Two is on suggesting how leadership skills are changing and on helping you to get strategically beyond the traditional "flash in the plan." To sculpt the Optimum Organization Zone, you need a dream, a team and a scheme!

Last, in Part Three we explain some important personal stances, skills, and strategies to:

- Help you advance your enhancement
- Help you deal with the emerging organizational people problems and problem people
- Help you and your organization win

We also provide specific strategies to employ when you are getting the short end of the new organizational "slap-and-stick" approach.

Finally, we provide a suggested Millennium Manager's Bill of Rights—an idea whose time is long overdue.

Our Philosophy

As authors, we are advocates for the restoration and nurturing of the value that current and future managers bring to the dance. We believe that managers can be helpfully involved without being consumed and can make valuable contributions without being cannibalized.

We have tried to create a "customer-oriented" book that presents direct, simple advice about the obvious and the not-so-obvious as the new role of management plays itself out in organizations. It is a checklist for people who understand that managing change is as useless and arrogant a notion as managing time. We try to offer a collage of suggestions and opportunities to invite you to be more inquisitive, more adventurous, and more participative in the unfolding drama of the new millennium.

For you, the customer, we have striven to combine substance with style, theory with practicality, insight with humor, controversy with optimism, meaning with metaphor, productivity with paradox, and helpful theories with practical tips. Each chapter contains a list of questions or suggested tasks (Action Exercises) to help expand your faith, hope, and clarity.

One

The Present Is Prologue to the Future: The Countdown Has Begun, Have You Noticed?

Everyone wants to land and keep a meaningful job that fairly rewards diligence, discipline, and good work. The obvious question becomes: What are the prospects of doing so?

Whatever the title—"downsizing," "rightsizing," or "decruiting"—staff cutbacks continue to be the corporate world's tool of choice for becoming competitive. It is difficult to pick up a newspaper without reading about another large corporation that will dismiss thousands of employees over the next year. What can you do? How can you protect yourself into the next century?

The key survival mode is positive projection: learning to look beyond the horizon with an optimistic perspective. Just as there are great threats in the current and future organizational climates, there are also exciting possibilities and opportunities. Some things are predictable; some trends can be easily spotted and reliably extended into the future. For example, the trend toward flattening tall organizations will continue. This trend will not proceed in a linear fashion, for some companies' will cut too far and find that they need to rehire some excessed workers. But the overall direction is clear and predictable.

What is not so clear is the intervention of earthquake political events or technological breakthroughs that might change the speed or even stop a tendency dead in its tracks. Who could have predicted the fall of the Berlin Wall, the unification of Germany, the breakup of the former Soviet Union, or the advent of a powerful three-pound notebook computer selling for less than a refrigerator? These events have had enormous ramifications for business in the global village. Regardless of these events, however, the information highway would have continued to emerge, and global competition would have increased.

The trick is that you have to get ready for the twenty-first-century organization that has not yet been invented. It will be shaped by two forces: some startling and unpredictable events and some things that you already know are happening. Information is exploding. Access to information is easing. Ownership of organizations is changing: employees are buying their own companies, multinational partnering is breaking down old paradigms, and change is speeding up. The alterations that are already upon us, coupled with the continuation of technological, business, and social trends, are reshaping the world of work so drastically that you must respond to what seems reasonable and retool your skills, career, and life. Doing nothing is just not a wise option. You have no choice. Get ready now! The first rule that Jack Welch, the CEO of General Electric, lives by is "Control your own destiny or someone else will!"[1]

We hope that you share our excitement about the possibilities. Every threat is an opportunity. Every technological advance brings the promise of a higher standard of living. Just remember—change is learning, and in the next millennium, you will have more opportunities to learn than you ever dreamed of.

In the rest of this book, we provide you with insights into what you need to do to get ready for the world of work in the twenty-first century.

1. Noel M. Tichy and Stratford Sherman, *Control Your Own Destiny or Someone Else Will* (New York: Harper Collins, 1993).

1

Realities and Readiness: Six Futuristic Work Behaviors

Airline ticket counter:
"May I have a round-trip ticket, please?"
"Where to?"
"Right back here if you don't mind!"

The "Weaning of America"

Want Ad

Wanted: Responsible, weaned adult, willing to take on new challenges with limited structure, guidance, and supervision. Willing to help other managers and executives in their struggle to understand what's going on. Have compass, will travel! Other organizational baggage limited to one small, carry-on sack.

Frank Ogden, the noted world futurist, has suggested that the single most important employee trait in the next century will be attitude.[1] He believes that your predisposition toward change, adventure, and risk will determine your success in the next century. He has suggested that recruiters will hire and organizations will promote on the basis of workers' "adaptability quotient," rather than their "intelligence quotient." When, he wonders, will the "adaptability quotient" show up on the SATs?

While Ogden's view may seem extreme, we concur that willingness to change will be one of the critical success factors in the next century. And as change accelerates, the successful leaders will be those who typically see opportunities in these disturbances, whereas those who see only threats will cringe, choke, and de-focus. Employees rooted in the old, rigid, industrial paradigms will have great difficulty making it. The "weaning of America" is upon us! You must be induced to let go—to give up the comfort of mother's (organizational) milk and to find another source of nourishment.

What You Already Know

- Middle management is an endangered species—out of work, out of time, out of luck, and out of touch with that fact.
- Most of what middle management has traditionally done is now obsolete (acting as gatekeeper and information processor), thanks to the computer.
- The destructuring and de-organization is well under way, leading to flatter organizational structures.
- Just as cable TV has changed the emphasis in TV programming from "broadcasting" to "narrowcasting," businesses have begun to "micromarket," realizing that any product draws different responses from different types of customers.
- Structures have become more organic and less rigid (e.g., skunk works, temporary project and product teams).
- The White Rabbit's prediction has come true: You must work even harder to stay in the same place, and if you want to get anywhere, you must run twice as fast!

1. Frank Ogden, *The Last Book You'll Ever Read* (Toronto: McFarlane, Walter and Ross, 1993), pp. 1–6.

- Outsourcing is the resource of choice.
- Employee participation by everyone in everything is becoming the norm, rather than the exception.
- The realization that all stakeholders are indeed customers is finally taking hold.
- In the global village, everything you do is affected by the shock waves of world events.
- Anyone, anywhere, is a potential competitor and customer.
- Workforce diversity is increasing.
- White male dominance is an endangered, en-gendered species in organizations.
- The "sue-bonic plague" is upon the litigation-happy American culture.

What You May More Dimly See

- As if the cleansing of middle management weren't enough, "baby boomers" are reaching middle age, further complicating the "career pileup" phenomenon.[2]
- In the information age, *place* loses its meaning as a defining work variable. Work will be wherever the hard drive is. Organizations won't be buildings and land, they will be ideas, concepts, and networks. Work, home, and recreation may all occur in the same location. Work will give way to connectedness.
- In a wired world, your future challenge will be to manage selection and training, development, careers, expectations, and performance as measured by customer satisfaction.
- Every piece of new technology creates some new jobs, kills some old jobs, and, more important, upsets some old organizational processes.
- Work mirrors life. Like society, organizations are becoming more violent. Every day some CEO announces the coming dismissal of thousands of workers—the organi-

2. Karl Albrecht, *The Northbound Train* (New York: AMACOM, 1994), p. 40.

zational equivalent of society's mass muggings or drive-by shootings.

- The euphemistic "downsizing" now begins with "age-sizing" (age-cleansing). The history, talent, experience, and skills lost through this process will take many years to replace while we relearn the obvious. Age discrimination is illegal, however, slicing out whole segments with bribes and shutdowns is not.

- The U.S. federal government, having no real competition, has become a huge, slow dinosaur. The system, as it has been constructed by the politicians (most of whom are lawyers), is, we believe, beyond repair. Elsewhere on the globe, governments are moving rapidly to outsourcing and privatization. But the United States is among the slowest to take this obvious route.

- Ironically, empowered organizations are often frantic, fearful, less humane places to work (the unguided missile effect).

- In horizontal and lateral organizational networks, hierarchies are obsolete.

Millennium Milestones or Millstones: Current and Future Organizational Trends

The dissimilarities between industrial-age and information-age organizational activities far outweigh the commonalities. Just as thinking in the agricultural age was in many ways reversed by industrial-age realities, most industrial-age organizational policies and practices are the opposite of those utilized in the information-age environment![3] Consider the following shifts from industrial-age (historic) to information-age (current and future) practices and how these trends might shape the future of our organizations.

3. Ogden, p. 8.

Organizational Shifts

Old Paradigms	*New* Paradigms
Bigness	Smallness
Stability	Change
Predictability	Uncertainty
Continuity	Flexibility
Hierarchy	Empowerment
Mass production	Specialty shops (often, paradoxically, mass-produced)
Hiring	Outsourcing, overtime, leasing or contracting
Production orientation	Customer orientation
Unionization	Independent contracting
Seniority an asset	Seniority a liability
Management	Leadership
Human labor	Automation
Middle managers	Computers
9–5 work schedules	Teleworking and telecommuting
Local	Worldwide competition for labor
Gold as currency	Information as currency

The trends we have described, both seen and suspected, are invalidating almost every old management theory thrust upon you. Now you must proceed along unknown routes without any reliable or appropriate guidance system.

Six Futuristic Work Behaviors

For Sale—Old Management Theory!

Affordable—price reduced; charming, private, quaint old multilevel, custom-built management theory; secure, executive neighborhood; beautiful exterior (recently remodeled), interior needs work; near public transportation; in close proximity to the best schools; 2000+

square feet; could look almost new; fixer-upper's dream; room for expansion; structurally sound but has limited view.

With the disappearance of reliable management theories, how can we predict which characteristics will be critical to enduring and prevailing in the age of 2000+? How will employees be hired and judged in the next century? How can you avoid becoming a twenty-first-century loser who feels victimized, who is unemployable and resistant to change because of the wrong attitude, a lack of information, severe dependencies, and skills grounded in the past? We believe that there are six important traits that will determine organizational success in the decades ahead.

1. *Adaptability.* Change elicits a natural resistance, but the ability to accept and even embrace the alterations that will continue to occur will be prized. The ability to adjust your perspective, approach, and behavior to new paradigms will become more important to successful employment, and employees who cannot or will not make the needed transitions will quickly become second-class citizens.

2. *Appreciation of ambiguity.* In times of change, the ability to deal with unstructured, untested parameters and to arrive at satisfactory conclusions is necessary. Some people hate ambiguity; others love it. Whatever your predisposition, your best interests dictate that you learn to appreciate and deal with a lack of structure. Those who can successfully cope with ambiguity will prosper. Those who can't or won't will be left in the dust. You must learn to see structure where none exists and to create it out of swirling events.

3. *Accommodation.* Working effectively in the future will require participating in more and more intragroup and intergroup activities. Solo decision making is becoming less of an organizational reality. Learning the group and interpersonal leadership skills needed to assemble the right group and to value different cultural, functional, and organizational interests will be invaluable.

4. *Accomplishment.* "Bang for the buck!" Millennium organizations in the year 2000+ will be even more achievement-oriented than today's companies. Getting things done will be the way of the world, and figuring out how to make a contribution and improve the way things work will be one of your passports to success. As telecommuting removes some people from the traditional workplace, people will be judged more on performance achievements than on style; keeping their level of performance high, year after year, will be the minimum for survival. "What have you done for me recently?" is an enduring motto for the future. Performance appraisals will have short memories.

5. *Access ability.* Getting information that your people need to reach the goals will be of increasing value. Clarity derives from accurate information, including a full expression of feelings. Extracting information that counts from the ever-expanding highway of data will enable your people to use their limited time well. Expanding your knowledge of personal and computer networks is extremely important. In the years ahead, you will have to know what you need, where to look for it, and how to retrieve it.

6. *Accessibility.* You must be available to your people. Accessibility translates into frequent and effective group experiences (meetings, project pursuit sessions), as well as intensive one-on-one time. The natural press of business encourages managers to distance themselves from their people. This separation will become very bad form. Accessibility is more than an open-door policy followed by a quick, polite rebuff. You must seek out your people. Help them get what they need. Provide support, information, and resources. Shield them. Share with them.

Skills, theories, and roadmaps come and go. In fact, a primary survival capability of the future will be the ability to cast off what you have learned. These six attitudes and orientations will allow you to take in information, make adjustments, learn new ways—and move on in this great adventure.

You must deep-six your old habits and traditional responses!

Action Exercise 1-1

How would you rate yourself on each of the Deep Six Factors?

	Great									*Poor*
1. Adaptability	10	9	8	7	6	5	4	3	2	1
2. Appreciation of ambiguity	10	9	8	7	6	5	4	3	2	1
3. Accommodation	10	9	8	7	6	5	4	3	2	1
4. Accomplishment	10	9	8	7	6	5	4	3	2	1
5. Access ability	10	9	8	7	6	5	4	3	2	1
6. Accessibility	10	9	8	7	6	5	4	3	2	1

List three things that you could do to help improve your scores.

1. _____

2. _____

3. _____

Action Exercise 1-2

Select three trends from this chapter that you think will have the most effect on your organization and on your industry.

Three Most Important Trends   Impact of Each Trend

1. _____   _____

2. _____   _____

3. _____   _____

Brainstorm how you could turn each potential disaster into an opportunity.

1. _____

2. _____

3. _____

2

Paradoxes, Paradigms, and New Possibilities

"Anything done to excess is toxic!"

Change is not necessarily progress, but progress cannot occur without change. Leaders have three specific functions in the change process: See it, focus it, and model it! While change, fast or slow, is the story of human history, the exploding rate of change in the 1990s has caused proliferating responses. (Does life mirror work, or does work mirror life?) Life in our institutions is undergoing a transformation that will ultimately produce the workplace of tomorrow. Some changes are conscious, natural, and healthy. Others are spastic and rooted in corporate diseases that strangle the life from the enterprise and are setups for future failure. One paramount question for the millennium is, "What upheaval lurks in the hearts of organizations?"

Why Things Aren't Working That Well: Organizational Dysfunctions and Disabilities

Having influence in the organization means understanding what is functioning properly and what is dysfunctional. Dysfunctional activities and processes must be understood on two levels:

1. The "overt" ways in which the dysfunctions occur, are displayed, and get acted out
2. How you personally are affected by and get hooked into participating in these dysfunctions

Examples of Dysfunctions

- *Shifting responsibility to others*—the global enactment of "It's not my job!"
- *Fragmentation*—the seeking of cures for big problems by breaking them down into their most minute pieces, reassembling them through some sort of balkanized logic, and energetically attacking the symptoms.
- *Conditioned independence*—the destructive side of competition, focusing on beating your own peers, resulting in a form of corporate cannibalism.
- *Learning disabilities*—the inability to trust, cooperate, co-ordinate, and/or synergize.
- *Shiftlessness*—the inability to see the dysfunctionality of basic old surface paradigms and the need to change them.
- *Motion sickness*—the urgent need to be in motion, not in thought, regarding crises, projects, and problems: "Show 'em we're on top of things."
- *Short-term-itis*—taking the shortsighted, quick-fix, band-aid view to solving the organization's long-term problems.
- *Spastic responses*—the traditional "Load, fire, and aim" mentality, a knee-jerk, shoot-from-the-hip, "do-something-even-if-it's-wrong" response that is usually exhausting and ineffective.

Navigating in Permanent Turbulent Waters

Water is symbolic of life, renewal, cleansing, and regeneration. Permanent white water (PWW) is Peter Vaill's metaphor of choice for a lasting condition of organizational life.[1] When water is funneled from a wide space through a narrow one, it is forced to pick up speed in order to displace more water in the same time. When this channeling is accompanied by a drop in elevation over uneven surfaces, the resulting turbulence creates "white water." This turbulent water condition, as a metaphor for business conditions, has become permanent, as managers quickly convert "rafting in turbulent water" to their own work experience: frightening, exhilarating, challenging, and overwhelming.

For American companies, business in the 1950s and early 1960s was placid and predictable, while Japan, Germany, Great Britain, and France struggled to rebuild their industrial furnaces. The worldwide demand for products exceeded the supply. The pickings were easy. Then came the industrial rebound, first from Germany, then from Japan. Turbulent waters began to appear in the external environment for U.S. companies.

Permanent turbulent water is no longer confined to the outdoors. The tempestuousness has seeped inside the organizations. In an attempt to steer and navigate in this global white water, organizations are now pushing reengineering, downsizing, outsourcing, and quality initiatives of all types. Competition, innovation, and technological change have created a fierce commotion in most marketplaces and in most organizations.

Ironically, at a time when the United States, building on social protections such as unemployment benefits and Social Security, has been debating the efficacy of national health care, the psychological work contract that many adult workers depended on has been reduced to a historical footnote. The death of organizational loyalty, coupled with continuous, accelerated change, is creating a flood of organizational events resulting in permanent white water conditions. The organizational luxury of quiet stretches of placid pools, soothing balmy days, regular respites, and long sections of competitive drifting are, historically speaking, way back upstream. And the pace of change will continue

---

1. See Peter Vaill, *Managing as a Performing Art* (New York: Macmillan Publishing Company, 1989).

to accelerate. Competition will intensify even further. And managers will be forced to learn how to navigate in the virtual reality of virtual turbulence.

A major roadblock to meeting the challenges of permanent turbulent water is the unconscious belief that this cascading ride will somehow end soon, that if we just hold on, all will soon be eased and softened. This mind-set, believing that the world will certainly slow down soon so that we can get off this pitching monster, translates into the wrong behaviors. People getting ready to get off have a different focus from people getting ready for the next shock, the next excitement. The training is different. The tools are different. Training for the permanent, turbulent water trip requires:

- Heads-up, continually searching behavior
- High-level sensing to raise and heighten awareness
- A relentless sorting of old data and assumptions
- Intuition, the ability to see over the horizon with accuracy
- Learning to live in the new paradise of paradox
- Staying grounded, focused, balanced, and in tune
- Remaining flexible and open

As turmoil increases, loose ends abound, and logic and magic come unglued, the traditional response of the executive mind and management culture has been to reach deep into the anthropological past and steer this thing hard! Management's approach has emphasized these tactics:

- Exhort ("Let's get organized around here!")
- Move out (linearly), and make something happen
- Gain control somehow and get on top of things
- Take charge, grab the ball, and run with it
- Think logically (and rigidly)
- Be systematic
- When in doubt, cut costs
- Use power or lose it

These hard drivers and hard strivers are the skeptics, cynics, realists, and "I-told-you-so" bunch who knew all along that the new wave of management thinking was just another passing fancy of a temporarily deranged executive suite. They have watched too many other noble efforts ebb and flow. They even perceive a cycle or rhythm to it all, usually lasting about five years. What is launched in fantastic fanfare fades fast in the light of a free-falling profit statement. The inherent incompleteness and flaws in their basic design and implementation usually doomed management by objectives (MBO), Total Quality Management (TQM), and all the other techniques from the beginning. The traditionalists are right: These "new" vaccinations never took. Equally wrong, however, is the fallback to the old, hard-nosed "kick-ass-and-take-names" tactics. They don't, indeed, fit turbulent waters.

Increasingly, it is becoming apparent that hard-nosed management works either poorly or not at all in permanent churning water conditions. "Hunkered-down, under-the-gun" employees haven't the time, confidence, or temperament to perceive the deeper, long-term needs or to anticipate what's around the bend.

The Paradox of the New Needed Guidance Systems

Turbulence requires new thoughts and new expressions of old thoughts. The millennium leader has to navigate permanent churning water using intelligence, intuition, insight, and vision. Nurturing and nuance are as important as numbers and negotiation. Leadership requires new paradigms, breakthrough experiences, and mental leaps that come from thinking upside down, sideways, and inside out while minding the seemingly irrelevant.

When John Naisbitt in *Megatrends* pronounced the coming era of "high tech, high touch," a collective "aha" chorus rose from the management ranks. It was seen as a cute, neat slogan that we must support. But to traditional management people, high touch means soft touch, touched in the head, or simply out of touch. The value of high touch is to be really in touch with the people and subtleties in complex environments. Managers responsible for people who are overworked and overwrought can easily overlook what's important. High touch means being close to people, their minds, their energy, and their processes. The true spirit of high touch, revealing more than hard data about trends, patterns, and markets is: "If it can't be measured, it is probably important!"

The "trick for treats" is to combine good, solid data with the flow of human intuition, insights, feelings, and needs. For managers to prevail, it will become more important to:

- Be sensitive but street smart.
- Plan your work and abandon your plan.
- Play it where it lies.
- Sit light in the saddle (or the kayak).
- Go with the flow.
- Improvise as you go.
- Use the current; don't fight it!
- Encourage everyone to steer (group steering is everyone leaning in the right direction).

Yet it is the paradox of management approaches that is the bicuspid of management power. Is the hard-controlling route or the gentle touch of open creative "people nurturing" needed? The answer is a resounding yes! Either oar is appropriate at different times. The deft use of both approaches is the sign of the master navigator.

Permanent turbulent water is causing some truly mind-numbing management afflictions:

1. Action gridlock:
   - Pure paralysis—since you can't predict the future, you can't act, producing the Buddhist Management Approach—don't just do something, sit there!
   - Management fibrillation, a random but furious activity with no constructive results.

2. Hardening of the categories:
   - Inability to see things that are new and different.
   - Requiring more and more energy to pump through any change.
3. Helplessness, hopelessness, and powerlessness:
   - Why fix anything? It will just come undone again—giving into cynicism and sarcasm.
   - Company misery loves company.
4. Denial and avoidance:
   - Fixing blame.
   - Positioning the sandbags.
   - Deflecting any responsibility.
5. Spastic programming and quick fixes
   - The illusion of instant cures, fads, and panaceas (zero defects, MBO, TQM, and continuous improvement).
   - Consultant-itis.

Of course, through all of this, some good employees get downsized, rightsized, and blindsided. Using slogans such as "cutting out the fat" and "tightening our belts," many leaders have been given carte blanche to reverse the excesses of the past and to either get the organization into fighting shape or kill it! Certainly, there is a great deal of fat in most large organizations, placed there by decades of empire building and permitted by distracted executives. The current practice of merge-and-purge would be admirable if it weren't often being done for the wrong reasons—to cover up the mistakes of the past and to punish the wrong people. Solid strategic questions help provide a guidance system in turbulent times. Some pertinent questions are:

- When is cutting helpful, and when does it dismember a finely tuned competitive machine?
- When is commitment powerful, and when is it blind?
- Is loyalty good when it is not reciprocal?
- When do "can-do's" turn into "thumb screws"?
- Would you rather be laid off on Friday or told to do even more with even less on Monday?
- Metaphorically, when does the level of difficulty of the

white water rapids exceed the capabilities of the boat and crew?
- When does exhaustion make further progress ill advised?

Navigational Guides

Successful navigation requires assessing the storms and potential hazards you will encounter en route. Look out for these areas of turbulence in your organization:

1. The organizational climate, which used to be positive, pleasant, or at least civil, has become hostile.
2. People are blaming one another for not carrying enough of the load. (The real problem lies at the top.)
3. Everyone is afraid to tell the "Supreme Empowerer" the truth.
4. Other departments are gaining resources, while your operation is losing resources.
5. Your leader is so loyal that he is a pushover for the top brass. He buys the "do-more-with-less" mentality so fully that they just give others more and him less.
6. People are playing the "we're-doing-more-than-you-are-with-less-than-you-have" game. These people haven't slept in weeks. Remember how unions got started?
7. Loyalty and "can-do" means everyone is afraid to express serious concerns about the plans. Remember that Dr. Deming suggested you must drive fear out of the organization?

In these turbulent areas, some of the players will be tossed overboard, some will jump ship for a more reasonable life, and others will die at their oars, adding a new phrase to our lexicon: "Dying more or less!" Sooner or later, the empowerer will strike again! To ensure your survival, learn to recognize these turbulent behaviors and gently refuse to play. If you can, get in and stop it.

Management Anorexia

The excesses we have pointed out so far lead us to a second
metaphor—a sad, growing, unhealthy cycle in many organizations that we call *management anorexia*. Organizations of all
shapes, sizes, and purposes, having binged on hiring in the past,
have entered an era of purging employees from the organization
through downsizing, even as the organization now binges on
empowerment and outsourcing. Ironically, the motive behind
the new wave of empowerment often is not a humane understanding of the dignity of the human worker but management's
wish to squeeze more out of everyone. Do you notice a pattern
here? Manipulating managers have turned a natural, periodic
cycle of readjustment into a crusade of lean-and-mean. It is in
fashion to show incredible intensity while in a self-denial mode.
Every job is a potential target for radical dieting or reshaping.
The survivors tend to be:

- Distracted by the events
- Insecure and fearful of future reductions
- Disloyal to the perpetrators
- Weary from the increased responsibilities
- Resentful about the anxiety

This behavior and its consequences have some of the same
common features as the illness anorexia nervosa. This widespread ailment produces:

- The joy of doing without (sacrifice)
- A gaunt and grim appearance
- A pervasive self-righteousness from self-imposed suf-
  fering
- An inability to perceive the disease or to alter its course
- An inability to readjust to a healthy balance

An emphasis on quality and continuous improvements has
the potential to make a profound difference in the long-term
performance of the organization. But in the anorexic environ-

ment, long-term learning, cultural accommodation, and skill building are supposed to be accomplished with fewer and fewer people running faster and farther while carrying their same old load plus the workload of every dropped-out employee. The tight faces and cynical comments combine to highlight management's lack of a true fix on reality, a common symptom of anorexia. Relaxed time is needed for creativity in developing concepts, experimentation, and proper training.

Often, during cost-reduction efforts, training and study groups meet on their own time, before work, after hours, or on weekends. One oxymoronic decision often made by management is to hold a power-packed weekend retreat to inspire the troops and to laud their increasing workloads and productivity. Then, on Monday, the normal timetable is again invoked. Management is astonished to see that energy is low and people are too irritable to focus properly. But in the fanatical fitness training fad way of thinking, if running five miles is good for you, then running twenty miles is four times better! What a favor we have done for everyone!

Doing more with less has a noble ring to it. Overdone, however, it sets the stage for breakdowns and inept performance. High-quality customer service calls for balanced, healthy people who exude caring, fresh, and sparkling tones. This atmosphere is hard to create when the workers are undernourished! In the long run, there's some hope for anorexic organizations. We predict that in these unhealthy organizations the purge will eventually pass, and, as the surviving employees begin to pass out from malnutrition, the binge of rehiring will begin anew.

Action Exercise 2-1

1. How unstable is the environment in your industry?

   Very Stable   Very Unstable

      1   2   3   4   5   6   7   8   9   10

2. What are the noticeable signs of permanent white water in your industry?

   _____

   _____

3. How is your organization dealing with these changes?

   _____

   _____

4. What is the potential for management anorexia in your organization?

   Very High   Very Low

      1   2   3   4   5   6   7   8   9   10

5. What are three implications of your answers for questions 1–4?

   1. _____

   2. _____

   3. _____

Action Exercise 2-2

Clarify the dysfunctions and obsessions in your organization as the starting point for meaningful organizational change.

1. Describe your organization's dysfunctions and obsessions.

2. Highlight the damage they do.

3. How do people collude to overlook and excuse these hurtful enterprises?

4. What could you do quickly to help your organization shift back to a more sane and sensible path?

3

The Challenge of Managing Meaningful Change, Enduring Truths, and Fads

"Meaningful change is fade-resistant!"

Change proposals elicit strong emotions, ranging from excitement to disdain to fear to confusion. One way to understand change is to see how people react. There are three common types of people.

1. *The zealots*—those employees who zealously and naively jump on any new bandwagon just so that they can appear to be on board and ahead of their time. The change serves *their* interests and meets their needs. They will energize the change, even if it's wrong.
2. *The "Bohicans"* (the deep bunker crowd)—those wise veterans of wars past who rally the troops around their battle cries of "bend over, here it comes again!" and "this too shall pass!" They have seen new programs, fearless fads, and searing systems come and go. In fact, for them, nothing lasts.
3. *The bewildered majority*—those caught in the middle, who wander around and are confused by both the zealots and

the Bohicans. They don't know enough to take a position and often resort to "I don't want to be involved."

Each of these employee types acts and reacts differently to proposed alterations in the organization. The zealots are dangerously agreeable and embrace any changes, the bewildered majority has a healthy resistance, and the Bohicans resist everything.

Resistance to Change Is Natural and Enemy Number 1

Resistance to change is a natural and sometimes useful, sometimes destructive process. The faster change occurs, the more resistance is forthcoming. (Resistance, of course, is the barrier to needed change and adaptation to the flow of reality.)

Why Resistance Occurs

- People lack the needed information.
- There are many different and possibly distorted perceptions about the change.
- People have never heard or accepted the reasons for the change.
- People have been kept in the dark about the change, and their natural fear of the unknown is agitated.
- People are risk-averse.
- People are exerting their power by resisting.
- People distrust the change agent (the zealot in charge).
- Workers are satisfied with the current situation.
- Employees want to protect their turf.
- People are merely saving face.
- Workers are giving in to peer pressure.
- Staff members have been conditioned by the organization culture.
- Subordinates weren't involved in planning the change.
- People believe the change is truly wrong.

The key question is: Where are you in regard to current changes? What do you need to have or to know before you can sign on?

Strategies for Managing Resistance

When you take on the change-maker role, you must know how to deal with natural and overdone resistances. Once you understand the many natural reasons for resisting change, you are better prepared to anticipate the types and amount of resistance.

Sixteen Ways to Manage Resistance

1. Create discontent with the way things are.
2. Clearly communicate the need for change.
3. Clearly communicate the goals of change.
4. Involve all interested employees in the planning.
5. Consider the individual needs of those affected.
6. Show a willingness to help people keep what they need.
7. Choose the most credible person to announce the change.
8. Allow for exceptions.
9. Encourage open exchange sessions for constructive venting.
10. Practice full disclosure to build trust.
11. Emphasize the areas of agreement.
12. Time announcements carefully.
13. Hold educational sessions on change.
14. Build new needed training and retraining into the plans.
15. Be open to changes.
16. Honor the resistance, expect it, and allow everyone some time to accept the change.[1]

---

1. Some of these suggestions were distilled from: Timothy Nolan, Leonard Goodstein, and J. William Pfeiffer, *Plan or Die: 10 Keys to Organizational Success* (San Diego, Calif.: Pfeiffer & Co., 1993), pp. 60–62.

These actions are cures for the problem of resistance. When done properly, they can reduce the life-cycle of the resistance and speed the implementation of change. Know these techniques, and manage them sharply.

Overcoming the Bohica Effect

The Bohicans are everywhere, in every organization. Bohicans are a subculture of resistance.[2] They lie in wait for opportunities to sabotage artistically the new efforts and then sit back smugly and issue their "I told you so"s! Most of the time, the Bohicans are a big pain. Occasionally, they can save your hide; more often, their extreme negativism eats at the organization like cancer. When you witness the Bohica effect in your organization, what can you do?

Ten Suggestions to Convert Bohi-Cans to We-Cans

1. *Don't start if you don't mean it.* A halfhearted program is worse than none at all. Damage control is expensive and extensive.

2. *If you started change for all the right-sounding reasons but ignored the unchanging human natures that would destroy it, give it up now.* Be honest about why you are quitting. Just repeat: "This takes a level of doing and thinking we can't handle. Sorry about that."

3. *Listen to your "people" people more and your "numbers" people less.* Don't start any new employee morale, culture change, or customer service things without doing your homework and getting expert advice.

4. *Write off the incorrigibles.* Some Bohicans never die, never fade away, and would complain about the food at the Last Supper. Move in, move on, and ignore them. They can't and won't be a meaningful, positive part of this or any other process. As

2. The section on overcoming the Bohica effect is based on our article of the same title published in *Business Horizons* (July/August 1994), pp. 2–4, by the Foundation for the School of Business at Indiana University. Used with permission.

you would write off a bad debt, write off certain segments of your management and workforce—and do what needs to be done.

5. *Avoid the self-fulfilling prophecy.* Don't manage this entire process as though most managers and other people are, in fact, doomed to be and act like Bohicans. That is compounding your mistakes.

6. *Size up the realistic impact of the Bohicans.* Remember, Bohicans pride themselves on their ability to poison the reservoir and then avoid the water. They spread incompetence, lack of confidence, and "party pooping" like organizational Typhoid Marys (or Martys!) Don't underestimate or overestimate their real ability to influence the outcome.

7. *Offer your best to the majority.* Keep them involved throughout.

8. *Don't give up what you really believe.* Don't give in to the Bohicans! Pursue your quality goals with the fervor, enthusiasm, and passion they deserve. If true quality begins to take hold, the Bohicans will be on the outside looking in.

9. *Change the reward system.* It is critical that the new quality initiatives be tied into the compensation system in meaningful ways. Remember, the job of the Bohicans is easy when management demands one thing while rewarding another. Any change that is not reflected in the reward system deserves to be classified as a fad.

10. *Defuse the Bohicans.* Anticipate the disgruntled rebuttals, and remove the obstacles, contradictions, and inconsistencies to demonstrate that this time and this program are different.

Bohicans collude! They often join in a negative force field. Understand them so you are not caught unprepared.

Enduring Truths: Then, Now, and Forever

In these days of changing, chaotic, upside down organizations, tough questions arise. What are the enduring management truths? What are the facts that were, are, and will be accurate?

What carryovers from the past are still true today and will be tomorrow? The following candidates are offered:

- Structure changes, but never really dies.
- The force of resistance to change weakens and strengthens, but lives on.
- Everyone craves affection and acceptance.
- Good long-term outcomes don't come cheap.
- Making it day-to-day is still what life is all about. Play it where it lies. Today is the first day of the rest of your life. The glass is at least half full. There are no guarantees. If you can't leave it, then love it!
- You don't own anything. You can't take it with you.
- Some diversity is always present. It's just not always seen, accepted, understood, appreciated, or given free rein. Managing any diversity requires diverse responses.
- How you care for casualties in organizational warfare is more deeply remembered than the cause of the casualties. All employees know that they may be candidates for tomorrow's "light casualty" list.
- It's much easier to get up in the morning and go to work when you work for a legend than when you work for a ledger or a lecher.
- What goes around eventually comes around. However, whatever it is it may have on a different costume.
- Prophets are the real bottom line.
- Ownership is magic.

Emerging Truths

Some new, about-to-be truths are now coming into focus.

- Travel light.
- Travel light in simple style, always ready to change direction or destination as mobility dictates.
- Plan, if only because planning focuses and facilitates.
- Abandon your plan when it no longer fits, regardless of the effort that has already been expended on it!

- You abandon your principles at great personal and organizational risk.
- Be wary of consultants, and use them well.
- Being a real, responsible grown-up is a heady experience, earned in joy and pain.
- Address all jobs as your own personal laboratory, learning clinic, and life seasoning.
- Nurture your bosses. If they have any soul at all, they know not what to do in these times. Help them in the struggle. Believe in them. They are in the same learning cycles that you are.
- Some people are the breath of death, evil in their self-serving destruction of those around them. Contain them. Expel them.
- Without hope, there is no hope. Be the center of hope wherever you are. More people care, hope, and give a damn than you might expect. Pay attention and locate them.
- Everyone wants to share in profitable performance.
- Extreme compensation packages for those lucky few in the executive suite are disgusting anachronisms and should be controlled now. They are part of the collusion among CEOs, boards of directors, and stockholders to bleed the last possible buck into short-run stock appreciations and dividends. We think it's better to emphasize long-term success and the value of the organization.

Managing the Hottest New Management Fads

Fads are practices that are born prematurely and tested poorly, often flawed and usually simplistic, followed for a short time with exaggerated zeal. Fads are quick, neat packages. What new management fad has been thrust before you? Empowerment? Rightsizing? Telecommuting? Re-engineering? Economic Value Added (EVA)? Paradigm shifting? Like knowledge itself, management fads are proliferating at a dizzying rate. Fads breed zealots and zealots breed fads, especially in the consulting

(Fads Are Us!) and lazy executive ranks—one size fits all, guaranteed to solve any organizational ailment. This mindless misapplication of sincere efforts is the bread and butter for many consultants and clueless executives. Knowing the answer before you know the question is standard operating procedure for self-righteous, ignorant fad-masters.

We don't know which is more dangerous, the illusion that some fad is an enduring truth or the truth that some enduring illusion is a fad. Many good management thrusts are emasculated by the fad label. While calling something a fad can kill organizational change, believing in the enduring nature of a fad can kill credibility. The organization loses in either scenario.

Types of Organizational Fads

There are three basic types of organizational fads: old fads, new fads, and recycled, repackaged fads. Old fads are fads that were once in vogue and are still being supported by some die-hard champions. New fads are ideas that appear to be genuine new approaches to improving quality, productivity, and performance. Upon closer examination, new fads usually turn out to be old wines in new bottles or new wines in old bottles, just plain recycled and repackaged. For example, the age-old idea of "doing it right" fell out of favor and was eventually replaced by the concept of "zero defects" (doing it right the first time), which has been resurrected as "total quality" (doing the right things right the first time). Obviously, these are potentially good ideas. In fact, good ideas are basic to good business. But they have been repackaged to reenergize short-term zeal. "Management by walking around" used to be called "getting out in the field." These recycled, repackaged ideas usually ooze into the organization through familiar routes. The idea originates from someone who has a vested interest in selling something—a business writer, a consultant, an editor, or a talk-show hostess. The idea is picked up by some executive who passes it along, suggesting or ordering underlings to "bathe the unwashed in the new elixir," which will surely pioneer the new path to organizational salvation.

The Fad Test: Does It Make A Real Contribution?

Some management strategies are decent ideas that can benefit the organization in many ways. Alternatively, as we have said, they may just be another fad. How can you tell? Test your suspected fad against these nine criteria. Do they:

1. Focus some new organizational tools and techniques on old, recurring maladies?
2. Bring some change to a stagnant climate?
3. Help to overcome inertia?
4. Provide an infusion of enthusiasm and effort?
5. Enable participation, involvement, and perhaps even commitment?
6. Lead the organization to focus on what's important?
7. Create space for creativity and innovation?
8. Admit that the status quo won't cut it?
9. Reduce "toil erosion"?

How can you turn a meaningful change but potential fad into a system-changing, inspirational new approach to curing old organizational ills? To nurture a good idea, try the following "magnificent seven" steps:

Strategies for Turning Potential Fads into Meaningful Changes

1. Ask for input from the key people regarding the new approach. If they respond positively, go on to #2.
2. Clarify what specific business problem the idea will cure.
3. Specify the true scope of the idea. Is it long range? Will it work in all situations?
4. Decide how the new approach will be tied into the compensation plan.
5. Discuss how everyone will be trained to understand and apply the new technique.
6. Investigate specific ways that senior management can exhibit support and provide visibility for the concept.

7. Build the new approach into all impacted systems and subsystems in the organization's operations.

Ironically, any process or idea in an organization can be viewed as a fad at some point. The trick is to make the idea part of the organization's culture so that suspicion is reduced and the appropriate behaviors follow. Fads are for real when they are *fade-resistant!*

Your Role as the Change Conduit

You always have dual, and often conflicting, roles. You are a changee and a changer. You toil under the changes made by others, and you make changes that affect others. Your job requires you to install and to instill changes, too. While you await the next change or are at work installing the latest installment, think about the changes you need to make in your own work, team, and organizational situation. These may be:

- New risks and breakthroughs in the way you do things
- Changes in outlook—yours, theirs, and that of the total system
- Changes in your own behavior and attitude within your team
- Changes in external relationships with clients, customers, suppliers, creditors, and other divisions within your company

When Should You Question Change?

How and when should you attempt to stop a group of employees who are "blinded by the light" and leading your organization headlong off a cliff?

There is a dangerous hypothesis taking hold in many organizations—the idea that all change is good and that anyone standing in the way is the enemy. Since most issues in a company are really change issues (e.g., time management, motivation), the dichotomy between meaningful change and fads and the problem of how to identify and manage them effectively become critical.

The expression "everything in moderation" is mirrored by the Asian concept of "balance" in life. This idea stems from the proposition that too much of anything is bad for you. When change starts sweeping through your organization, are those in charge throwing out the baby with the bath water? Is the change meaningful? Does it supplant an enduring truth? Is it just a fad? The dilemma for the manager is that excitement and passion are sometimes necessary for an idea to work. But when a group of newly converted zealots starts naively down the path to salvation, anyone standing in the way is seen as the enemy. Questioning the change is something akin to heresy. The honest thinker is subjected to cries of "Traitor," "Disloyal," "Negative," or "Paranoid!" (Remember, you're paranoid only if you think they are out to get you and they aren't.)

The material in this chapter should help you to shape a balanced view and a flexible response. Your organization's future and your own career could be at stake. Meaningful change? Enduring truths? Fads? In the final analysis, you must decide whether you are with the change or not.

Action Exercise 3-1

1. What is the biggest potential new fad in your organization?

   _____

2. Name three good things that this concept is encouraging.

   1. _____
   2. _____
   3. _____

3. List three destructive outcomes from this idea.

   1. _____
   2. _____
   3. _____

4. What three strategies might you be willing to try to help turn this potential fad into a more meaningful change?

   1. _____
   2. _____
   3. _____

5. If you were convinced that this technique was destructive and must be stopped, what might you do?

   _____

Action Exercise 3-2

Consider changes that you want to initiate or accelerate in your team and/ or organization.

1. List a few risks you want to take or breakthroughs you want to make.	2. What changes in your organization's outlook do you want to influence?
3. What changes do you want in your team's behavior and/or communications?	4. What changes in your external relationships with clients, customers, and suppliers can you make?

Action Exercise 3-3

We challenge you to come up with five enduring management truths that were true, are true, and will be true in the next century in your organization.

Enduring management truth 1:

Enduring management truth 2:

Enduring management truth 3:

Enduring management truth 4:

Enduring management truth 5:

Two

Creating the Optimum Organization Zone (O-Zone)

"As with athletes, there are rare, precious times when an individual, team, or organization performs at another level, truly performing in a zone that no one else is even vaguely familiar with."

As an organization dweller, perched on the edge of the new millennium, you may have some doubts about what to do, how to help, how to make a difference. Part Two outlines some changing skills and special perspectives you will need to make an impact, or perhaps just to survive.

The future successful organization must be able to create its own unique Organization Zone (O-Zone). There are three distinct but related levels of O-Zone-ness leading to the sculpting of the optimum Organization Zone. Each of these three pieces is uniquely applicable to each organizational setting.

The Three O-Zone Levels

1. The skill level of the people who manage and lead in the organization. *These skill components are changing. They range from direction setting and creative problem resolution (vision making) to*

more interpersonal functions—building the dream team, hooking everyone into the dream, and etching the clarity. At this level, the O-Zone can be artistic in its symmetry and inspiring in its clarity. The ongoing process requires strategic thinking, spearheaded by vision shaping, values, clarity, and an externally focused mission. These basic managerial skills are necessary but not sufficient to create the optimum O-Zone.

2. The information and energy exchange field with the outside world. *This O-Zone provides a permeable shield that surrounds the organization. The stronger the O-Zone layer, the less vulnerable the organization becomes. It can be strengthened through the genius of competitive advantage brought about by inspiration, passion, technology, or simply an atmosphere in which people are free to create and to question the status quo.*

3. The creation of a widely understood set of feelings, thoughts, and values that become almost a spiritual bond and experience. *This is the highest level, the one leading to the Optimum O-Zone. If in no other way, it is understood in organizations where there is a sense of organizational passion and "soul." Organizations do have souls, too, not just as a collection of individuals but as a separate, collective unit. Organizational souls can be vile and evil or inspiring and interesting. Level 3 is the intersection where common sense, common purpose, common good, and common spirituality converge. This third-level Organization Zone is a mental, physical, and spiritual state where truly exceptional performance becomes easy and natural. Consider the analogy of sports. Athletes often speak about being "in a zone" where:*

- *The batter sees the baseball as if it were a large grapefruit moving in slow motion rather than an aspirin tablet thrown at one hundred miles per hour.*
- *The basketball player sees the hoop as being much larger than it really is and can't miss a shot.*
- *The hockey goalie perceives the puck to be much larger and moving more slowly than it is in reality, making it easy to stop a shot by an opponent.*
- *The team reaches a level where it functions like the fingers of a hand, effortlessly, expertly, and beyond the capabilities of any other team.*

In the same way, when the organization has a truly inspiring vision and highly trained people, it has the potential to reach the third level where it is "in a zone" where the competition can't stop it but can only hope to contain it! The few organizations that reach this status become the Wizards of O.Z. They are not merely organizations but legends whose brains, hearts, and courage transcend those of mere organizations.

Now that we have established the growing importance and changing nature of the O-Zone in our organizations, what do you need to know to succeed? Four specific skills are basic to future organizational success:

1. Making the dream. *Managers, professionals, and leaders must have* strategic skills, *designing the dream and building the means to achieve it. Without a scintillating vision, there is neither excitement nor commitment. Managers at all levels are being asked to help decide the destination and to create the means of getting there. We don't need more paint-by-numbers managers; we need more leaders and more dreams.*

2. Building the dream team. *The global nature of business and the changing composition of the workforce are forcing managers to become* proficient team leaders *of a more diverse workforce. Leading a multicultural group is much more challenging. To prepare for this shift, you must be aware of when to use a group, how to build a team, how to use cultural differences, how to value the contributions that each makes to the total organization, and how to help the team when it gets stuck!*

3. Hooking everyone into the dream. *Organizational success will be determined by the ability of the managers to* motivate. *Different kinds of employees are motivated in different ways. You need to learn how to: manage those employees who are motivated by external incentives (this is often analogous to pulling teeth), inspire employees so that they motivate themselves (similar to pushing on a rope), and manage motivated people (much like the task of herding cats).*

4. Etching the clarity. Communication skills *have always been crucial to success. As turnaround times decrease and flexibility increases, the ability to communicate effectively grows even more in significance. To communicate well, you must be straight with yourself, your people, your customer, and your organization. Even as electronic*

capabilities explode, the need for more intense and deeper face-to-face communications expands. Etching the clarity also means that you must walk the talk—you must show what you know through your behavior. Finally, the manager of tomorrow will have to be a teacher, bestowing on others what she or he has been taught.

4

Making the Dream

"Dreams huddle closely with fantasies and halluci-nations! A real dream, though, can pull us into a desired future!"

The dream-personal is the foundation; enhancing your dreaming capability is the developmental task; a steady pulse of dreams that visualize desired futures is the output. Dreams are essential for individuals, sub-sets, and organizations. Organizations should encourage active dreaming and weave those dreams into future thinking and behaviors.

Building a truly living organism that is in continuous transition and transformation is too important to leave solely to the CEO, his or her direct reports, and other major leaders. In spite of big-buck bonding for them, it is too great a task and burden. Executives can't totally shape the magnitude of dreams that our cascading world requires. Dreaming the future needs to be a grassroots explosion as well as a top-of-the-tower task.

The future will bring tremendous turnover in focus, organizational design, and people. The same units, with the same folks doing the same tasks over a long period of time, will be rare from now on. Such "churning" requires the widespread fertility of new dreams and new ideas.

Vision making is underrated, overwritten, and currently suffers from a very bad image. Organizational image making is often left to "spin doctors" and public relations staff, whose task is to convert the unkempt, uncommitted, and unaccomplished into some bright, sassy blast of light. The paradox of visions is that you have to invent the future of your choice, knowing that no matter what you do, it will become its own thing. If you put energy into it, see it, massage it, it sort of becomes reality. Vision is such a rapturous paradox that we like to expand the idea to dream making! Dream making is an exotic science, a mixture of magic and logic. There is an art form to making things happen that everyone else says can't be envisioned, let alone accomplished.

Another paradox about the dream is that most people love exciting dreams but feel threatened by dreamers, who are cut from different cloth. In times of paradox, we laugh at things that we don't understand. But it is a nervous giggle, poorly hiding our fears.

Odd Images of This Dream Thing

Before we look more intently at dream making, let's ponder some curious ideas:

• The kaleidoscope may be a more appropriate tool for seeing the future than a telescope, horoscope, periscope, or microscope.

• If you really want to avoid vision making, then just pick up the latest copy of "generic visions for the directionally impaired." But generic visions are like paint-by-numbers; they have no soul! Books with prepackaged visions are easily found.

• Face facts. It is a great source of embarrassment to say you don't have a vision statement.

• Most vision statements, if done at all, have the same impact as this quarter's budget revision in prose form.

• Nothing is so poorly understood as the task of defining the desired place to be five or six years down the road.

• Focusing future pictures requires hard work and a gigantic leap of faith.

- Shapes become visible through vision.
- Dreaming should not begin with the onset of pain.
- Since there are few true visionaries (sorry!), most visions are a collective summary of hopes, energies, and possibilities.
- If you envision it and build it, they will come—attracted by its magnetic pull.

Question Finding and Question Framing

Whether it's your personal dreammaking group or organizational dream making, the key is finding what to ask. When the situation is chaotic, fear rules and gossip dominates. Whoever can apply clarity of thinking amid the confusion has the best chance of finding the most wonderful solution. Culling the useful information from the growing mass of data will be a prime skill. Solving your customers' problems better than anyone else demands that you be able to find the right questions and frame them in the right ways. Avoid the either/or kinds of questions, which create boxes.

Start with the basics: who, what, when, where, why, and how. For example, you might ask:

- Who are we?
- Who do we want to be?
- Who are our customers?
- Who are our competitors?
- What will we do better than anyone else?
- What is the prioritized order of our stakeholders?
- What do we value as an organization?
- What's really important here?
- What's slowly happening to us that we don't quite perceive?
- What will success look like?
- When will we become the dream?
- Where should we focus our resources?
- Where do we want to be in one year?
- Where is that felt need for change coming from?

- What things don't we feel free to question?
- Why do we stop ourselves from doing what we know should be done?
- How can we tell that we have achieved the vision?
- How can we separate the real problems from the symptoms and avoid becoming symptom addicts?

How To: Dreaming, Visions, and Designer Paradigms

The typical weakness of corporate dreaming is that it is a non-corporatewide event. It should be a thing done by individuals. The person in charge, and all those others, must have two things: first, dreaming skills and a commitment to do dreaming, and, second, a dream-in-the-making, one that is well under way, unfolding, and never done.

Let's look at what it takes to make designer dreams, schemes, paradigms, and possibilities:

- Action dreaming ("visioning") requires an attitude, a burly bias that believes that visualizing future events works, and works well.

- It also requires a belief that we do, in fact, affect future outcomes by the way we think about them. It works in finding parking places and in curing serious illness. The mind makes things happen, and the outcomes would be different if we didn't.

- This dreaming stuff is a hope-filled enterprise. It flies in the face of bad news, twists of fate, and the failure of our politics and global economics. Dreaming or visualizing a future is based on the ability to believe in a different and far better world than the one we live in now. Hard work activates everything. Built on a solid, deep-felt dream, it will work even better.

- Dreaming demands that you focus on *what really counts*. To paraphrase one of Robert Fulghum's wonderful stories, he was criticized as a young man by a seasoned soul as follows:

"Your problem, Fulghum, is that you don't know the difference between a lump in your oatmeal, a lump in your throat, and a lump in your breast."[1] Dreaming-for-impact requires working on what's important in every area of your life.

• People become that which they spend time thinking about and imagining. This explains why the miserable, the sad-sacks of the world, never get it sorted out.

• "It was always in there; I just released it." The sculptor will often say how easy it was to create a masterpiece—it was there, I simply extracted it, gave it a natural birth. It is the same for your possibilities.

The Vision Hierarchy

The problem with the corporate vision is that it is done at the corporate level. Do the ideas just presented look like the work of a board of directors or a senior executive team? That, of course, depends on the character of some of those key players and how much freedom they feel they have to reach out and imagine all over the place.

The Individual: The Seat of Dreams

This is the place where it happens. Dreaming/visualizing is a personal thing. The goal of every organization might be to reward people not for their skill at reciting the corporate (vision, mission, song) but for how well they can dream their own competence, their accomplishments, their next vista. In his book *A Force of Ones*, Stanley Herman talks about the individual's need to develop power in order for the organization to have anything to work with.[2]

---

1. Robert Fulghum. *Uh-Oh*. (New York: Villard Books, 1991), p. 146.
2. Stanley M. Herman. *A Force of Ones: Reclaiming Individual Power in a Time of Teams, Work Groups and other Crowds* (San Francisco: Jossey-Bass, 1994).

The Team Dream

If the power of dreaming for organizations lies with the person, the lone, sole individual, it is in the collection of a few people in the core team that it can be converted to a collective effort. Some thoughts about that:

• *The need for a believer.* It really works best if the leader of the team/group has some feel for and faith in this dreaming thing. Since it is so unusual, it takes more than a bit of courage even to bring it up.

• *"What if"ing.* A nonthreatening way of getting dreaming onto the team agenda is through the "what if" process. The proof is in the capturing of a "what if" born of wild imagination. Once started, and done again and again, the possibility becomes real to others on the team.

• *"Dream storming."* Team meetings become more vital when the whole agenda now and then is given over to floating dreams by each member and then linking them together. This process matures as the team practices the meeting for dreams. It is slightly different from brainstorming because it is a constant process of the participants. Day and night, the subconscious focuses on the next possibility, the next mix of ideas, products, services, solutions.

The Network Dream

As the group gets bigger, the power of the dreaming process becomes harder to put together. If, however, we can teach simple group processes such as brainstorming, nominal group technique, and mind-mapping to work groups, we can also teach barrier-busting, mind-shifting, paradigm-popping dream techniques to the same audience.

Not everyone will want to do this. The ability to see beyond the horizon, to shape the unforeseeable, is not now widely held. There are not many who can dream well; they are sprinkled here and there among the networks of teams. Like democracy itself, not all things that are inclusive have full representation—can't and shouldn't. In the same way, a dream task force of those who like to dig deep into themselves and push the edges can be formed and worked.

Forging dreams among networks of teams in organizations is a new idea. It is a step beyond the collective making of missions and the typical vision statements that lack fire and focus. The rules are to be made up as you go along:

- Encourage pushing the edges.
- Be aware of the parallel realities of staying in business while reinventing it.
- Try anything that works to stimulate the dreaming process.
- Invite others into dreaming.
- Understand that dreams take shape behind our daily activities, over time, day and night. They will pop out, again, day or night, when we least expect them.

The Corporate Dream

At the top of the dream hierarchy is the corporate dream, the realm of gossamer wings. Realistically, it probably doesn't work often, except for small, entrepreneurial groups. Big groups would have to plug into a cosmic consciousness that few understand, believe in, or can work in—for now. All the attempts to collect the ever-loving "input" from ranks below, by their nature, usually don't work.

The visionary person can make this work for a while and can surely make a positive difference. Visualizing for powerful changes, however, is done best at the individual or the small-group level. The dreams concocted there can form the basis for strategic shifts and cultural turn-arounds. "Dream shopping" may be the most important thing that the CEO or division chief can do.

Dream Making: Organization Style

Here are three dream suggestions to get you thinking:

1. *The ecstatic customer.* Dream the perfect service or product. Imagine the customer getting the contribution from whatever you do at the most exotic level, exceeding all expectations.

2. *The perfect partnership.* Imagine the most synergistic relationship, blending talents and technology at the highest levels. It may not even exist, which is the dreaming part. If it doesn't exist, how could you create it?

3. *The research of choice.* Imagine the flow of great insight, patents, techniques, and technology to ensure the constant regeneration of the business. What would that be? Where might that be located? Who can trigger that for you?

Dream Making: Personal Style, Career, and Work

The Appraisal Milestones

This is an invitation to write your own performance appraisal ten years from now. Begin by setting up the criteria you think will be important then. The dream will have to imagine new organization focuses, new forms, new opportunities, and new technology all around you. How will you contribute? How will you be involved? What will be asked of you? What will you ask of yourself?

Next, fill in the features with your delivery within those criteria. Dream, too, about who is making those assessments: yourself, your team, your customers, your suppliers (an up-link and down-link look). As you create these frames to fill, you will trigger thoughts, visual pictures, and possibilities.

The third step is to do this framing and filling at the five-year mark, half the time to the piece you just did.

Last, shape the frame and fill in the blanks for just a year from now.

Take a look at the pattern. How do the performance appraisal and the characters around it change over time? How does dreaming help, and how does it trigger deeper dreaming?

The Rolling Resumé

The experience of painting in your appraisals-future can tell you a lot about the organization you may inhabit. The rolling resumé is another method of structuring the dreaming process. Write down your own detailed resumé for ten years from now. What will you record as the experiences that have flowed through your life? What core competencies will you have found, used, moved through and beyond? How will you reflect the breadth and depth of your career? Who can you report as references who understand who you are? How will you be a major contributor to the life and good works of your organization?

Next, take this to the five-year mark; repeat it for next year. How does the focus change (or stay the same)? Is there stretch and imagination? Do you show the effects of visualizing the possible?

The Life Dream

People who deliberately decide to dream about their future personal lives make the quickest, biggest strides. Again, we tend to become that which we think about. The more vivid the picture, the more it hardens into a reality and the more our energy moves that way instead of toward other attractions and distractions. The categories of quality of life are many. Putting them into the dream process is a deliberate act. You can think about:

- *A life partner*—love, warmth, shared journey. Who, where, when, and how will it look, feel, be?
- *Joy index*—what will be your life turn-on? What turn-offs will be purged?
- *Excitement, challenge*—how will you jump into the new, vital, interesting? Who will that be? What circle of friends?

- *Spiritual, religious, universal connections*—where are you in that journey? What might the destination be for you?
- *Physical accomplishment, whole health, a fresh, fluid energy, and good feelings*—what might they require?

Dream Making Needs a Lonely Place

You can do anything you want to do in life; you just have to pay the consequences. If you think envisioning the future is tough, try living with the results when you don't anticipate the next tidal wave. If you think planning is useless, try (like Alice in Wonderland) getting somewhere when you don't know where you are going. Often, the vision-maker is really the lensholder, positioning it, twisting it, and holding it for everyone to see. Many people may have cleaned and polished the lens. When properly shaped and aimed, the light that the lens concentrates will burn away resistance, complaints, doubt, and skepticism. But when you first start this mystical vision-thing, you will be different, alone, a target.

Dream-Killer 1. The Cliché Catalog for Nonstrategic Dreamers

Many people are averse to planning. As the management guru Peter Drucker has said, they plan Tuesday all day Tuesday![3] Over the years, nonplanners have offered a ton of lame excuses for not planning. While mostly inane, perhaps the exercise makes them feel less guilty. We herewith offer some of our favorite reasons for not dreaming—the "Cliché Catalog for Nonstrategic Dreamers!"

3. Peter F. Drucker. *Management: Tasks, Responsibilities, Practices.* (New York: Harper and Row, 1974), p. 35.

The Cliche Catalog for Nonstrategic Dreamers

Cliché	Translation	Obvious Question
Dreaming takes too much time.	Let's plan Tuesday all day Tuesday.	How much time does firefighting take?
We tried it, but it didn't work.	We sabotaged it from the beginning.	Did you quit riding your bike after you fell?
Our industry is too different.	I'm scared.	Isn't that what every industry says?
If it ain't broke, don't fix it.	We might dream wrong.	What if it's about to break?
Dreaming isn't practical.	I'm knee-deep in alligators.	Why not drain the swamp?
The top people won't go for it.	I can read minds.	Wouldn't any change be better than this?
Let's study the idea.	That should kill it.	Is overcoming inertia that tough?
It costs too much.	They might find me out.	What is the cost of doing nothing?
What does the typical firm do?	Let's be mediocre.	Why not lead?
We've done well improvising.	I don't know how to dream.	Humans have always walked; why fly?
My boss needs this stuff.	Don't expect me to take any risks.	When did you first notice the pains?
Dreaming can't be done well.	There, now I don't have to deal with it.	Is that why we were able to land on the moon?

A commitment to dream making and dream building is not always fun and games. Commitment means being psychologically, physically, and emotionally impelled to make something happen. The Kamikazi pilot on his fiftieth mission is involved but not committed. Committed people will do what it takes, find a way! Commitment comes from a clear vision and individual ownership. We have already discussed the need for an exciting, scintillating target. Ownership in the strategy process is equally necessary. To make this point quickly, how many times have you seen someone wash a rented car?

Dream-Killer 2. Benchmarking: Accepting Imitation for Inspiration

One of the hottest topics of the 90s is benchmarking—studying what other, successful companies have done in a particular area and implementing these actions in your own organization. The good news is that benchmarking can improve your organization by upgrading your operations. The bad news is that copying what others are doing or have done is not very creative and creates equality, rather than superiority. Why not assign two groups to work simultaneously on improving a particular function? One group will strike out on its own to create and invent a new way to operate, with no prior constraints; the second will benchmark the best examples of successful organizations. When completed, compare the findings of the two groups. What can be integrated from both efforts to make your process even better?

Adding It Up

Dreaming is the difference between existing and living, mediocrity and greatness. Without dreams we become robotic sleepwalkers. Whether it's personal, team, network, or organizational—when done properly, dream making stirs the imagination, gets the juices flowing, and focuses the energy. Yesterday's dreams can become today's possibilities and tomorrow's reality. Seen any good dreams lately?

Action Exercise 4-1

1. What large changes have taken place in your industry?

2. What smaller changes may have gone unnoticed?

3. Are you sure you know what business you are in?

4. How clear is your organization's vision?

5. How well have you communicated the vision in your shop?

6. How much competition will you face in the next five years?

7. How clearly have you identified your internal strengths and weaknesses?

8. How recently have you analyzed the external opportunities and threats?

9. Do you have the resources needed to make changes to increase your success?

10. What could interrupt your income (sales, revenues, grants, etc.) in the next five years?

Action Exercise 4-2

Looking to the future, what do YOU have going for you and what do you need to develop? (list and describe)

1. What are your personal strengths?

2. What are your weaknesses?

3. What skills will be needed in your industry in the future?

4. How well do you match up with what is going to be needed?

5. What can you do in the next year to improve your chances for success?

Action Exercise 4-3

Looking to the future and your organization's intentions as expressed in the vision and values, what does your organization have going for it, and what does it need to develop?

1. What are your organization's strengths?

2. What are your organization's weaknesses?

3. What are the organizational opportunities, and how might you respond to them?

4. What are the threats to your organization, and how might you respond to them?

Action Exercise 4-4
Hard-Thinking Log

Successful people make the time to dream and think hard. If you could spend quality, uninterrupted time each day (or at least each week) thinking about your organization and yourself, both would benefit greatly.

Try to carve out thirty minutes a day for dreaming/thinking hard. Keep a log to provide incentive.

Monday:

Tuesday:

Wednesday:

Thursday:

Friday:

Saturday:

Sunday:

5

Building the Dream Team

*"Can you build a great team with
six flavors of vanilla?"*

Now that you have a scintillating dream/vision, how are you
going to build the team that can deliver on the promise? Do you
even need a team? Would a loose group of talented individuals
suffice or even surpass?

Here is a paradox: You need a great team of people with
diverse skills to perform a symphony well, but no team has ever
written a great symphony!

Groups or Individuals? Let's Get
Ready to Rumble

Most people have strong feelings about working alone or in
groups. There isn't anything magical about using an individual
or a group to solve a problem. This may sound like heresy in
these days of "courageous leaders" and "empowered teams,"
but, like most things in life, the truth is somewhere in between
these extremes. Don't let the overzealous crusaders suck you
into the quicksand. Groups aren't always the appropriate
problem-solving unit. Neither are individuals. Sometimes we

would trade all the meetings for one visionary leader; at other times, we would like some input into our futures. It depends. To butcher a phrase, "You can empower some of the people some of the time, but you can't empower all the people all the time." Some employees have had about all the empowerment they can stand. Our firm hope is that the powers that be will do some of their own work and quit dumping all of it on us. The reality is that there are many conditions that support a group decision, and many that support an individual decision.[1]

Ten Instances When Groups Are the Best Choice to Advance the Vision

1. When you will need to have the commitment of the group's members to have any chance at successfully implementing the decision.
2. When there is no clear expert on the problem or the solution is sprinkled among many in the group.
3. When your organizational climate supports group efforts.
4. When you have the luxury of a lot of time to make the choice or when the outcome is so vital that it is worth the time needed to work through groups.
5. When the people want to be empowered.
6. When different kinds of expertise are needed and must be coordinated.
7. When the people in your organization have had some training and experience in the art of collaboration.
8. When the problem has many parts that are suitable for a division of labor.
9. When the costs of a wrong decision are the main concern.
10. When you have been ordered to do so. Be sure to earn group members' trust by telling them the facts and asking for their input and help to make the collaboration work.

1. These criteria supporting group and individual decisions are an expansion of those found in: Judith R. Gordon, *A Diagnostic Approach to Organizational Behavior,* 4th ed. (Needham Heights, Mass.: Allyn and Bacon, 1993), p. 241.

You are much more expert about your own organization than we are. There may be special instances or circumstances in your operation that would encourage a group decision. Brainstorm these, and add them to this list.

The instances in which an individual decision might be superior are almost the direct opposite of the circumstances that favor a group decision. An individual problem-solving effort is usually superior to an individual decision:

Ten Instances When Individuals Are the Best Choice to Advance the Vision

1. When commitment is not critical to implementation because you have a great power position or the decision doesn't affect other people directly.
2. When one individual is the true expert in the area of concern.
3. When the organizational climate is individualistic.
4. When there is not enough time to go through the group process for problem solving.
5. When people would rather be left alone than be empowered.
6. When a unique kind of creativity is needed.
7. When the people in your organization are mostly competitive, can't overcome competitive motives, and competitiveness is distorting the shape of decisions.
8. When efficiency is needed.
9. When the costs (in time or salaries) of making the decision are the main consideration.
10. When you have been ordered to do so.

Once again, examine your own organization and experiences to cull some additional instances unique to your shop that favor individual decisions.

What Does a "Team" Look Like?

When was the last time you saw a team? How did you know it was a team? Was it the uniforms? Was it the interconnected nature of members' roles? Was it their common goal? While it is not easy to put into words, there is something special about being a member of a well-functioning team.

We propose the following definition for the dream team. This is our modified version of the definition found in Katzenbach and Smith's *The Wisdom of Teams.* Read the explanation carefully, because it helps to explain why some teams never become cohesive units.

> **The Dream Team has from three to ten people, focused on a common target, with interconnected roles, complementary know-how, a self-created process, and a "committed connectedness" that holds all members mutually and equally responsible and accountable for the results.**

Chicken or Egg?

Do you need a dream team or a team with a dream? Ah, there's the rub! Perhaps cause and effect are out of whack. The ongoing ability to explore "what ifs" in a significant way can keep the dreams coming and the power and energy in the group flowing freely into new things. Nothing is more sought after, more theorized about, more debated (ad nauseam), and more slippery to grab and hold onto than this thing called a "team." Why does something that sounds so great fall so flat so often?

Organizations of the future will be quick-moving, adaptive, temporary systems organized around "hot spots" that will be diffused by groups of relative strangers with different professional skills. But beware—groups can either be built into highly effective teams or become obstacles to progress that reinforce conformity and kill individual initiatives.

Built-in Blocks, Barriers, and Illusions

Standing in the way of effective team building are:

• *The top-down flaw.* Autocratic demands to make and do this team thing impede teamwork. Teams don't thrive in a control-down, dictatorial atmosphere.

• *The individualism barrier.* At some core level, this whole push for teams is "un-American." Team members have to overcome deep-seated cultural norms and decades of conditioning about doing it all yourself. We admire the star, the individualist. We yearn for independence—not much of a team framework.

• *The Great Athlete hang-up.* We "blubber on" with our sports metaphors as the sole learning and inspiration pieces for teams. Sports metaphors can be effective with the right audience, but they can also present several problems. For example, the inspirational videos by sports heroes such as the football coach Lou Holtz and the former football star Fran Tarkenton typically get "wows" from almost exclusively male striver audiences. Good stuff! But not necessarily the right stuff for the business team settings of tomorrow.

If you can't develop any scintillating examples except through sports metaphors, at least utilize a variety of sports. Are all your team members familiar with the sports favorites you choose? Which sports would your team most like to emulate? Do you want team meetings to be like a rugby scrum? Field hockey? Baseball, with its competitive nature and pastoral elements but also inevitable waiting, chewing, scratching, and spitting? Football, with its carefully divided and integrated male roles and socially acceptable on-field violence? Soccer, with its low scoring, continuous action, and spectator violence? Or perhaps a fist fight where a hockey game breaks out? All sports have something to teach us. In fact, by merely talking in your group about each person's preferences in the sports world, you will learn a lot about members' biases about sports teams, and you can preview some of the obstacles you will need to overcome.

Some Realities About Teams

There are some simple truths about teams that are worth noting. They include these points:

• Tough tasks help focus teams best. Teams without challenging goals quickly disintegrate into former teams. But merely filling the dumper with a long list of tasks won't cut it, either.

• Teams run poorly in neutral. To get your team running hard, entice members into the "dreaming mode," reflecting on ways they can actually make a difference. Magic *may* (not *will*) happen.

• The life of a team is more like a pulsing heart than a "pedal to the metal" race car. There is a real ebb and flow. The cycle looks like this:

> • We learn to get with this "team thing."
> • We get space to dream and invent.
> • It works, and we do good things.
> • There is a relaxed time, a breather. The good news is that learning and celebration can now take place.
> • Now for an encore: a fresh dream!

The strident worriers at the top get very nervous over this cycle. They want a full-bore, unrelenting charge. Well, quite honestly, that's a bore, too.

• Some groups can't ever get it together.

• The groups that succeed will "fly high" for a while and eventually let up (per the cycle just described).

• Some people working in the same small space have absolutely no need for each other in performing their daily tasks or for support. To them, team building is the result of some misguided leader somewhere trying to change them for some unseen and unrealistic reason. Their suspicions and frustration grow with each passing effort.

• Some group members usually never make the transition to teams, much less dream teams, because they come to the group for the wrong reasons, with the wrong agendas and the wrong approach.

• Teams don't have groupies! A groupie hangs on and around for emotional support. There is a high-level social motive and a need to "vent." The result is a vast waste of time and energy on side issues.

• Teams in organizations don't have spectators. (Dream

teams have admirers.) Have you ever been to a two-hour meeting where only one or two people spoke the whole time while the others nodded their heads and grunted agreement? Didn't they look a lot like those dogs with the bobbing heads you sometimes see in the rear window of a car? Didn't you feel as if you had wasted the two hours? To avoid this, don't call people to a meeting if you don't want to hear what they have to say. Encourage everyone to speak out. Balance the toning, tuning, and timing. Let those who aren't contributing know that they are missed, but don't just stifle the others. And dis-invite yourself to the meetings where you can't be heard.

• Group think impedes the search for truth. The truth should be the goal. When group members are caving in to the wishes of the group leader or a dominant member, a team is not possible. As first explained by Irving Janis, groupthink creates premature answers to ill-defined problems, answers signed off on by the group in a false sense of cooperation.[2] Whether the leader wins such acquiescence by playing on the group's adulation or fear or by relying on his or her own charisma or expertise, you can't pursue truth in this environment.

• Teams are very effective at creative conflict and personal challenge. In fact, dream teams encourage individuality, blended in a creative atmosphere. Individual insulation, insolence, and insincerity are the ingredients for a classic dose of disaster!

The Raised Bar

How about a track metaphor? In team high-jumping competition, the bar keeps going up. In true team stuff, the bar starts fairly high and, yes, goes up.

• Trust, openness, and caring are inputs, not outputs. You have to risk early and go forward. Waiting out every member to see if he or she deserves your trust blocks the outcome. Sorry, that's the way it is!

2. Irving Janis, "Groupthink," *Psychology Today* (June 1971).

• Groups, teams, and people all operate on at least two planes at the same time.

> • *Task activities*—the effort of the group to define a problem, plan an action, shape an idea, sort out facts, and set priorities is mostly a left-brain, thinking kind of operation. Good teams do this well.
> • *Process activities*—good teams "function" well together. "Process" gets attention when someone asks, "Are we straying from our purpose now?" or says, "Most of the talking is being done by two people; what does that mean?" Process has to do with how things happen—collapsing issues, calling for closure, checking out where the energy level is, and stopping people from "zapping" others.

• In true teams, members become committed to one another's goals and issues to the level where "if she doesn't make her goal, I have failed!" In "extreme team," each person is a consultant to, and a confidant of, others. There is a shared accountability for dream seeking and for individual effort.

Valuing Workforce Diversity

Dramatic shifts are occurring in the composition of the traditional workforce. Many organizations, mired in the old ways, are not prepared to utilize the diverse human capital of women, people of color, and older and disabled workers. Those organizations practicing exclusionary behaviors will be particularly dysfunctional in view of the shifting cultures and the changing makeup of the workforce. For example, changes in the demographics of the United States population are leading to an increase in the number of Hispanic and Asian workers. It is estimated that 85 percent of the net increase in the U.S. workforce will consist of women and minorities by the year 2000.[3] The

3. *Workforce 2000 Report,* U.S. Department of Labor, 1987.

number of older workers will also increase as baby boomers age and mandatory retirement is eliminated.

How can organizations better utilize the new talent pools to become more productive and more profitable and to improve morale? There are four important aspects of managing diversity:

1. Focus on understanding the new diversity of values, goals, and needs among each of these groups.
2. Overcome the tendency to stereotype groups, because there are great differences within each group.
3. Learn to value and celebrate diversity.
4. Offer all employees equal opportunities to develop their skills and talents.

To realize the complementary contributions of diverse groups to organizational success, try to:

- Include on both permanent and temporary teams people from all levels, experiences, age groups, and functions within the organization.
- Use empowerment to help reduce the natural barriers to members' reaching their full potential.
- Provide training and development to assist advancement.
- Provide flexible work arrangements to respond to different preferences and life needs.
- Eliminate discrimination: Recruit, select, evaluate, and promote strictly on the basis of performance.
- Devise creative strategies that will allow employees from all backgrounds to succeed.

Beyond Cultural Diversity to Cognitive Diversity

A truly critical type of diversity that is often overlooked is personality. Stereotyping hides the fact that each of us is the same, only different. For example, employees might vary from *internalizers*, who believe they control their own lives to *exter-*

nalizers, who believe others control their lives;[4] from *Type As* (competitive, prompt, impatient) to *Type Bs* (relaxed, expressive, with a longer time perspective);[5] from *introverts* (who are shy and withdrawn) to *extroverts* (who are outgoing and aggressive); and from *outline*-oriented (enjoys thinking in broad terms) to *detail*-oriented (wants to see all the particulars).[6]

Each personality has its own tendencies and uniqueness. To manage diversity successfully, you must be sensitive to the differences within groups and account for them in your approach to each individual. The organization needs diversity to prosper. Each personality type brings strengths and weaknesses; together, they provide the coverage needed to deal with problems successfully and in more complete ways.

The Team Gradient

We believe that there are levels of "teamness." Our hierarchy looks like this:

• *Mobs.* Mobs are characterized by high energy, irrational conformity, short life, and intense focus. Mobs may have a dream, or at least a fantasy. Mobs are of limited value in organizations, and, if you join one, you had better pick your spot well.

• *Groups.* Groups are managed (or mismanaged) in traditional ways with modest expectations, the usual game playing, and high casualty rates. Those who get the ax are shown through the friendly use of performance appraisals to have failed as individuals.

• *Teams in the midst.* Here and there in the hierarchy, management tolerates, encourages, supports (or has failed to notice

4. J. B. Rotter, *Generalized Expectancies for Internal Versus External Control of Reinforcement.* Psychological Monographs 1, no. 609 (1966): 80.
5. M. Friedman and R. Roseman, *Type A Behavior and Your Heart* (New York: Knopf, 1974).
6. Carl G. Jung, *Collected Works,* ed. H. Read, M. Fordham, and G. Adler (Princeton, N.J.: Princeton University Press, 1953).

and stop) some people who are seriously building team norms and trying to make them work. Teams can sprout in hierarchies that are low on punishment, low on fear, and benign in leadership.

• *Teams of dreams.* A few groups take on a life of their own, with members nurtured by progressive leadership and inspired by one another, their work, and their accomplishments. They need special protection and space and will operate differently from team to team and even vary in the way it functions over time. On one level, their learning about themselves inside a team experience is part of why they do it in the first place. When this team happens, be cautious about replacing team members, and keep great projects available to it.

As a guide in assessing the degree of team-ness achieved by a group, we offer some markers to look for (and, perhaps, to look out for—because they are indicators of powerful things going on). You may want to add scales to the following two checklists and use them as measuring devices.

Checklist 1 The Extraordinary Behavior of Team Players

- Help others meet their goals
- Ask for help
- Know the overall vision and care about it
- Carry water for and to one another
- Anticipate needs
- Give lots of positive feedback
- Think like team owners and general managers
- Fight with colleagues when needed and use the creative energy found in conflict
- Talk often with one another and with members of other teams
- Take the initiative and take risks
- Trust, then verify
- Practice full disclosure
- Have a sense of humor
- Celebrate and have fun

Checklist 2 Things Empowered Team Members Do

- Grab core issues and sculpt them
- Know what will make a difference and do it
- Display urgency and intensity about things that count
- Identify critical changes that are needed
- Directly oppose bad ideas
- Recognize leadership needs and either fill them or demand that they be filled
- Think and act like management
- Insert themselves into issues that affect them
- Speak up, talk straight, and question when needed

The Failure of the Self-Managed "Anything"

Self-managed teams can work, especially in organizations that have no more than three people. Once there are more than three people, it is inevitable that someone wants to push things ahead while someone else isn't ready, and someone else wants things to move ahead as long as he doesn't have to do it. As noble as the concept sounds, being part of a free-wheeling group (often unfairly and prematurely called a "team"), managing itself fully, is something that most human animals aren't ready for. We truly wish that the driver of the move toward self-managing groups were a wish to free the human spirit to innovate and forge deep connections with customers. But, alas, the driver is most often the genesis of current, common organizational strategy: more bang, less bucks, more wins, less losses, with the generic urgencies we have all come to know and hate.

Melding Generational Differences

Creating a team with multiple generations has its own built-in problems. While the following categories may border on stereotyping, we believe it is informative to view the "common prime directives" of each generation of employees. There are some interesting clues that point to ways each group is a little different from the others because of its "imprinting," and these differences have implications for how you might initially approach them.

The 1950s. Most of the people who went to work in the 1950s adhere to the motto "Serve the organization!" These workers are basically hard workers who believe in loyalty and in putting in a hard day's work for a fair day's pay. They grew up during World War II, "the good war," where good and evil were clearly defined. The 1950s were a time of great economic prosperity in the United States, and life was black and white, just like the television programs.

The 1960s. Those who were entering college and, later, the workforce during the 1960s were taught to question authority and were confronted with a time of uncertainty, the assassination of a president, the civil rights movement, and the Vietnam Conflict that was tearing the country apart. Their teachers were more leftwing politically, more liberal, and the motto for many young people became "Screw the organization!" Living through the Vietnam War (the war we tied or lost), this generation is often unfocused.

The 1970s. Those workers who joined the organization ranks in the 1970s were more Machiavellian than their predecessors. Disillusioned by the events of the preceding decades, many of these individuals believed that "self-service is what benefits the organization."

The 1980s. Perhaps the most arrogant group, many of the workers who entered the workforce in the 1980s took the stance "They're lucky I show up at all!" Ironically, this attitude prevailed at a time when American products were being hammered by Japanese manufactures.

The 1990s. As tremendous losses in market share and rising costs led to huge corporate downsizings, workers joining the labor force in the 1990s have had more realistic attitudes—"God, I hope I can get in. They promised me that if I worked hard, kept my nose clean, got an education, I'd have a job." "I'll work hard for you because jobs are tough to find and tough to perform, but don't hassle me too much or I'll call my lawyer or start my own business."

The "Aughts" (2001–2009). Predictions of behaviors we're likely to see ten years from now have become the norm for right here and now. How can you get ready to manage in the years of the "aughts" (2000, 2001, 2003, and so on)? The contract between organizations and the people who live in them has been dissolved. The parent-child relationship, harsh parent and nurturing parent alike, is coming undone. The shift away from the boss as parent strands the employee who still seeks the strong leader role because he or she will be dependent. Prepping for tomorrow is now the permanent task of every employee, and the fear that we won't be good enough, strong enough, or resilient enough haunts us all.

So what will be the nature of workers—of ourselves—as we enter the land of aughts? First, the people of aught-land will want clear and straight contracts with the employer. They will operate as private consultants/contractors, and having all the elements of the relationship made clear will be essential. Wild promises of prospects that no one can visualize, much less guarantee, will poison the connection even as it begins. The people of aughts will be in search of family—the warm, small team family of the past. This will increase the pressure on real, close-knit, private-life families. Work will no longer be the family experience it was for many.

At the same time, work and private life will rub together, and erecting the boundaries to avoid too much contamination will be difficult. No one, thanks to electronic nets, will be far from work. In fact, we will return to the journeyman era in that each of us will have our own electronic tool kits at home or in the car. The dramatic counterpoint of extreme interdependence and intense connectedness with work will confuse and excite.

Aught folk will understand that the essential investment is the investment in self, and the measure of worth is core competence. Stretch, growth, and divestiture of outdated skills will be the major effort. Because of the tension inherent in always being temporary and on the move, the ability to stop, recharge, and take stock will be a major ingredient in individual well-being.

The key to melding different generations of workers together is to treat them the same, only differently. It's a matter of style and of providing for their disparate wants and needs. Just as coaches of sporting teams have had to adjust their styles over time to their players and the new realities, you must learn how to approach each group on its own turf. There is real power in what groups can teach each other.

The Growth of the Generic Careers: Flowing Through Multiple Teams

The sense of who we are in the matter of work will undergo dramatic changes as we pole-vault toward the year of 2000+ and the decade of the aughts. We may still gain entry to the first organization stopping-off point by having some set of functional skills: computer skills, or skills in accounting, engineering, production, statistics, and so on. However, the transferability that is necessary for the future will require generic thinking about generic careers.

We suggest that the security of the future will lie in thinking about work as a career, not as a place where work takes place (i.e., a company or government agency). However, the definition of career should include some functional output, not simply a general field, such as human resources, design, or research.

A Starter List of Generic Careers

- Problem solver
- Facilitator
- Learner/teacher
- Expert project tracker
- Mediator
- Catalyst
- Entrepreneur, business maker
- Creator/generator
- Human energy motivator
- Healer, health maintainer

Generic careers take a particular orientation and attitude about them. They have their own expertise and technology in different endeavors, but they are fundamental in their differences. Generic careers focus on outcomes—the differences that result because the work was done well.

What to Do When the Team Breaks Down

Even the best assemblage of people can get bogged down in the organizational mud and spin its wheels. When the team breaks down or gets stuck and starts acting stuck, try these tips to help get things moving again.[7]

1. Create disenchantment with the way things are. (This may sound strange, but you need to create an atmosphere in which change will be welcome.) Pain often drives team stuff!
2. Return to the dream. Remember the old Russian proverb—repetition is the mother of learning.
3. Keep the need for change in front of the team.
4. Generate some fresh, creative ideas, facts, information, and perspectives. Involve the team in that search often!
5. Achieve some small, attainable victories, and celebrate them.
6. Change the team leader.
7. Change the team membership.
8. Bring in a talented facilitator to get the team's attention turned back to the vision, mission, and performance.
9. Repackage the rewards for team success.
10. Identify extraordinary team play, and play it up.

Hierarchy Just Won't Go Away

Part of the problem in building a team is that hierarchy just won't go away. Maybe it will in Millennium 3000. In the midst

7. These suggestions build on the set presented in: Jon R. Katzenbach and Douglas K. Smith, *The Wisdom of Teams* (Boston: Harvard Business School Press, 1993), pp. 160–163.

of the cries for leaderless teams (currently called "self-managed work teams"), there is always the hovering shadow of hierarchy. We believe in the power of the "extreme team," smart groups that shape goals, plan actions, and creatively solve problems on the way to goal achievement. But it will serve you well to remember that all of this takes place in the context of hierarchies. These hierarchies are natural to the human experience and include:

• *Hierarchies of experience.* Some of us get more, deeper, and sooner than others. We all share in having experiences; we just don't all have the same kind. Nice thought, isn't it?

• *Hierarchies of vision.* Some people can see beyond a boundary, some can see beyond several boundaries, and a blessed few can see into other dimensions. Some people can see beyond the horizon, and some can't see beyond the water cooler.

• *Hierarchies of talent.* Yes, mother, some people would rather do it themselves. Some don't want to, don't know how, and never will.

• *Hierarchies of learning.* In the learning organization, each person will learn different things at different times, and some will go faster and deeper and have greater ability to apply their learning.

• *Hierarchies of development.* Maturity is a marvelous condition to seek, and we are all in varying stages of development. But while you are only young once, you can be immature forever. People evolve, over time, in context, and when they are ready. When you suggest that a teammate grow up, he may take the advice or take offense. People who believe in reincarnation might say, "Well, maybe next trip."

• *Hierarchies of preferences.* Each of us likes certain things and dislikes other things. We discriminate among stimuli. Whether our likes are politically correct or political-pleasing may be in the eye of the beholder. We like certain types of people more than others. It's natural and will not go away.

• *Organizational hierarchy.* The old, proverbial hierarchy. Of course, no matter how "self-managed" a team is, someone else in the organization has a vested interest in the outcomes, and so does that person's boss. And so it goes.

Issues of Constancy and Consistency

A culture of self-responsibility and "people maturity" takes time to develop and needs nurturing to sustain. Organizations, with their futuristic "flow-through tea bag" structures, can't seem to keep a division intact long enough to make the self-managed part work. The constant dissolution and divestiture of organizational units discourages such efforts.

Furthermore, consistent, long-term reward systems that support self-managed processes are not here yet. Total systems revisions are needed; even when they are in place, teams still must overcome all the other obstacles we have discussed.

Adding It Up

The team thing is here to stay. Ignore this fact at your own peril. While teams have great potential to change and improve the workplace, teams are often:

- Poorly done
- Created for the wrong reasons
- Filled with false starts
- Never, ever, truly finished
- An experience done unto someone (and the command is issued—"You will form a team tomorrow!")
- Simply proclaimed into existence. Since this announcement comes through the same channels, in the same tones, and with the same crisp deadlines as the most recent across-the-board staff and budget cuts, it's hard for those affected to be enthused.

In spite of all this, there really isn't a choice. If those who demand teams understood what they were really asking for, they would start the process of team development and play it out differently. The litmus test is always the same—"For real? C'mon, man!"

Organizations can become "fields of dreams" or minefields. Once the vision is set, you must decide which parts are best handled by individuals and which parts are suited for team-work. If you want to create dream teams, then recruit the right members, train them in "teamness," remove the roadblocks, share the dream, and get out of the way. The "dream team" is a collection of diverse experts with mutual respect and responsi-bility, committed connectedness, and a team dream. Meld the differences! Value the diversity! Just remember—there is a fine line between dreaming and hallucination!

Action Exercise 5-1

This self-analysis form is something that nobody can honestly fill out.
Look at the categories, but do not complete the form. Realize that deep
inside, we have prejudged many groups and are biased against their efforts.

How would you rate each of the following groups on industriousness?

(Circle one for each category)

	Extremely Industrious									*Extremely Lazy*
Asians	10	9	8	7	6	5	4	3	2	1
Western Europeans	10	9	8	7	6	5	4	3	2	1
Eastern Europeans	10	9	8	7	6	5	4	3	2	1
Middle Easterners	10	9	8	7	6	5	4	3	2	1
American Indians	10	9	8	7	6	5	4	3	2	1
White Males	10	9	8	7	6	5	4	3	2	1
White Females	10	9	8	7	6	5	4	3	2	1
Black Males	10	9	8	7	6	5	4	3	2	1
Black Females	10	9	8	7	6	5	4	3	2	1
Hispanic Males	10	9	8	7	6	5	4	3	2	1
Hispanic Females	10	9	8	7	6	5	4	3	2	1
Age 21–30	10	9	8	7	6	5	4	3	2	1
Age 31–40	10	9	8	7	6	5	4	3	2	1
Age 41–50	10	9	8	7	6	5	4	3	2	1
Age 51–60	10	9	8	7	6	5	4	3	2	1
Over 60	10	9	8	7	6	5	4	3	2	1

Did you rate the group you belong to the highest? Why?

Action Exercise 5-2

Focus on the changes you want in your team.

1. What do you want/need from the formal leader?

   • Do more:

   • Do less:

   • Keep on doing:

2. Look at one team member who is critical to team play. What do you want from that person?

   • Do more:

   • Do less:

   • Keep on doing:

3. What specific behavioral changes do you need to make to advance the team's performance?

   • Do more:

   • Do less:

   • Keep on doing:

Action Exercise 5-3
The Extreme/Dream Team

How can we increase our support, caring, and concern for each other?

What do we need to give ourselves permission to do?

What is the level of our "team spirit" right now?

What are we currently doing that is counterproductive in our work?

Which people on our team need to work together more closely than they currently do?

What is the nature of our individual and collective work load, and how can we make helpful adjustments?

How can we build better working relationships?

What makes you most proud here?

How do we think "too small"?

6

Hooking Everyone Into the Dream

"Don't use the rack approach to employee growth."

At this point, you should have developed a great dream/vision and selected the individuals and dream team to make it happen. Now, how are you going to get everyone on board and hooked into the exciting pursuit? You will need to meet people where they are! Different categories of employees should be motivated in different ways.

Managing the Three Aspects of Motivation

The art and practice of motivating people has been evolving over the past few decades. This evolution will continue in the new millennium. In the not-too-distant past, managerial motivation skills were almost entirely derived from the answers to two questions: "What motivates people?" and "How does the process of motivation take place?" If optimum people performance is the goal, how do we achieve it? Managers used education (reading books, taking classes or seminars), modeling (watching a great motivator in action), or coaching to unlock the secrets to motivating employees.

There are three aspects to motivating people: using external rewards and discipline, hooking self-motivation, and, newest and perhaps most interesting, managing motivated people. The first aspect, emphasizing ways to motivate others, is still the prevailing concern in autocratic organizations, but the importance attached to this concern varies according to the progressiveness of the organization, its management philosophy, and the skills of the employees. For those organizations stuck in the autocratic mode, the manager's time is still mainly consumed with figuring out how to motivate people. But even for these archaic organizations, the question has taken on new meanings as middle management and organizational loyalty disappear and employees, coworkers, and customers cease to be only English-speaking white males.

The movement in organizations is more often toward the second aspect of motivation—building self-motivation. In this phase, motivation evolves from "How do I get Jack to be more productive" to "How do I get Jack turned on so that he motivates himself?"

The final aspect of organizational motivation is the prevailing mode in most new, progressive organizations, where the dominant question is: "How do you manage a motivated person?" As more organizations "go horizontal" and "empowerment" becomes the norm to maximize human intellectual capital, the leaders' quandary changes from "How do I get them going" or "How do I turn on their internal generators" to "They're all off and running; now what do I do?" As Frederick Herzberg suggested decades ago, most managers do not understand how to manage motivated employees.[1] But as the wise Chinese general Lao-Tsu suggested: "I must find out where my people are going so that I can lead them there!"

Since motivating people, getting people to motivate themselves, and managing motivated people are all still parts of most managers' jobs, we explore these three issues in this chapter.

---

1. Frederick Herzberg, "One More Time: How Do You Motivate Employees?" *Harvard Business Review* (January/February 1968): 53–61.

Dealing With Frustration

If you want to engage yourself in this motivational arena, you should first check out your frustration coping skills. Frustration happens! Frustration is easy to develop, hard to deal with, and simple to explain. Frustration is just anxious discontent. Most frustration is caused by one of two events:

1. A goal is blocked (you can't get there from here).
2. There are competing or conflicting goals (you want to spend more time on your career and more time with your family).

Do these sound familiar? Maybe the plane takes off without you! Your promotion gets nixed! You miss your daughter's championship softball game! Your boss and your spouse are both mad at you because they want more quality time! How many times have you been frustrated because you were trying to do something that was being thwarted, trying to do too much, or simply unaware that you were trying to accomplish two conflicting goals?

What to do? The answer is simple. As the doctor said when the patient complained that his arm hurt when he did that, "Don't do that!"

Frustrated people act out five common behaviors. They may:

1. *Lose it and go ballistic.* The possibilities include: attacking the cause, yelling at an innocent bystander (passerby, spouse, or kids), and beating up some inanimate object, such as a pillow.

2. *Go back to the good old ways and days.* People sometimes assume the fetal position, sucking their thumb and humming old, comforting songs.

3. *Get out of there.* Leave, retire, daydream, or become quiet and nonresponsive.

4. *Keep beating their heads against that proverbial wall* (metaphorically or literally).

5. *Problem-solve constructive solutions.* People can gain a new awareness, find a new way, change the goal(s), or clearly establish their priorities.

Which action above do you think is most productive? Which action is most humorous? Once an employee is able to get into a rational frame of mind and look for possible solutions, he can usually solve his own dilemma.

Your job as a manager is to help people to see objectively the blockage or conflict that is causing the frustration and to find an appropriate answer—unless you are the one that is frustrated because you can't get some employee to do what you want. In that case you should close the door, throw a dynamite temper tantrum, and then proceed to list the possible solutions, prioritize them, and choose the best one. (Now you know why some Japanese companies have special padded rooms where managers can go to have cathartic experiences.)

An Organizational Explanation of Motivation

The explanation of motivation in the organization begins with a dream, as discussed in Chapter 4, and quickly moves to organizational and employee goals and needs.[2] What does the organization want to happen? What does the employee want to occur? The closer the match between organizational and employee goals, the easier it is to motivate.

The organization transmits its goals and needs through its reward system. How closely do the rewards being offered match the rewards sought by the workforce? Another contributing factor is the organizational issue of corporate culture and the credibility of immediate supervisors. Does the employee trust the boss and the organization to do what they say? If so, the employee will be willing to exert a lot of effort. This effort will,

2. Parts of this explanation are based on the approach found in: L. W. Porter and E. E. Lawler, *Managerial Attitude and Performance* (Homewood, Ill.: Richard D. Irwin, 1968), pp. 165–166.

of course, be affected by the employee's abilities, the working conditions, employee training, the equipment being used, and how clearly her role is perceived by the employee. If all is well, the performance will be good.

After performing well, what rewards does the employee receive? Was the reward fair compared to those received by her peers? Was it fair considering the amount of effort that was needed? Was it fair considering the "opportunity costs" of what the employee could have been doing with her time and effort? If so, the employee will be satisfied and willing to perform well again. Just remember what the psychologist Abraham Maslow taught us through his hierarchy of needs—as needs get filled, they lose their motivating value. Unfilled needs motivate best!

Pulling Teeth: How to Motivate People Externally

How do you get someone to do something that he or she isn't doing now? Some employees respond to external motivators. The good news is that "How to get people to do what you want" is a dynamite topic to study and discuss. The bad news is that there have been hundreds of books and thousands of articles published on external motivation, and we still don't seem to be motivating really well. Our own business observations have led us to conclude that understanding how to motivate and the practice of motivating don't seem to be directly related in the real world. There is apparently a huge difference between knowing motivation theories and actually being able to motivate anyone. When it comes to motivation, you must be able to show what you know! Walking the talk is tough stuff!

When you witness an employee doing something that puzzles you, remember this—normal people do what brings them more pleasure and/or less pain. It's that simple. Unless the person is psychologically unbalanced (if you suspect this, call in the experts), she is doing what she has consciously chosen to do. When a behavior is puzzling, it is because you do not perceive the options the same way the other person does. In the person's mind, this behavior was the best choice. Once you understand and accept this premise, seemingly puzzling behavior becomes easier to understand.

Employees are the same, only different. Some consequences (such as money) are attractive to almost everyone, although to varying degrees. Other consequences (such as responsibility) may be perceived as pleasant or unpleasant, depending on the employee. Your job is to talk with each of your people and observe each person's behavior in order to learn what he finds appealing and what he finds distasteful. To motivate people externally, you provide what they want in exchange for what you and the organization want. Think of it as moving someone from the "no-zone" to the "go-zone"!

The external motivational process needed to get employees to do things includes:

- Establishing clear goals
- Clearly communicating the goals
- Understanding what your people want and need
- Providing rewards that satisfy those needs
- Giving clear feedback on performance
- Rewarding fairly and consistently
- Reviewing the process and making needed changes

The skills needed to accomplish this motivational sequence include:

- Goal setting
- Clear communications
- Objectivity
- Expert application of external rewards
- Information sharing
- Conducting a solid performance appraisal

Make sure you avoid the "Snap-Back Syndrome," in which you try your best to get someone to do something; then, when the person still resists, deflects, acts up, or does poor work, you "snap back" to your traditional style and force compliance, thus setting up a self-fulfilling prophesy for the worker—"See, I told you they don't care" (translation: "They didn't mean it!").

Classic Failures in External Motivation

The organizational graveyard is crowded with stereotypical failures to motivate properly. Most organizations have reward systems that encourage behavior that is counterproductive to the total organizational performance. For example, how do you think auto mechanics will behave when they are paid on an incentive system based on the total price of the new parts they install? Their behavior will be unethical at times, won't it? Won't the mechanics prescribe and perform unnecessary work? Whose fault is this? When production workers are rewarded according to their cost reductions and salespeople are rewarded by sales, what happens when an important customer wants a special (costly) run of certain items? Will production and sales cooperate? Why should production do it? When the first person into work in the morning has to make the 150-cup pot of coffee, don't you think some people will be encouraged to arrive late? When a frustrated boss takes the easy way out and transfers a poor performer to another department where the morale is great and the tasks more challenging, don't you think that poor performance has been rewarded? There are thousands of examples of an improper application of rewards in organizations.

Pushing on a Rope: How to Get People to Motivate Themselves

As you can imagine, worrying continually about externally motivating every employee is extremely time-consuming and not the best use of managers' time. Besides, true motivation is an "inside job"! Wouldn't it be nice to get your people turned on so that they motivate themselves? How, you ask? The answer is simple. What would make someone take care of things without being told? The answer is the same psychological factors that makes management work long hours and, usually, work hard to do its best. These internal motivators have always been, and always will be, job-related items (such as Herzberg's motivators)—control, responsibility, achievement, recognition, growth, and interesting work.

Control is a powerful motivator. If you own it, you will take care of it. But if management owns it and you are just a hired hand, then why should you be as concerned?

It is necessary for management to give up some of the power and to empower the employees to take care of things in their own way and when they think they should. Scary stuff? Not really. Remember that people protect what they own, not what they rent. If I value control, as most people do, I will exercise great care to see that I don't lose it!

The skills needed for getting people to motivate themselves are:

- Creating an exciting vision
- Clearly delegating responsibilities
- Trusting people fully
- Committing time and money to develop employees
- Shaping and sharing power to encourage a "free-flow zone"

Be forewarned, however: Getting people to motivate themselves is like pushing on a rope—it's their decision.

Herding Cats: How to Manage Motivated People

When an organization has shifted from trying to motivate its employees to turning the employees on so that they motivate themselves, management must ask itself what its role should be. The skills needed for managing motivated people emphasize coordination, collaboration, creating a climate of risk taking, and taking advantage of personal charisma and conceptual charisma (skillfully using intellectual arguments to persuade).

When it comes to managing those who are motivated, the dream thing and the team thing are both cause and effect. For those who are inner-driven, having a chance to shape and chase a vision is an exciting experience. The team is the forum through which that happens. Once involved in the process, such workers reveal their excitement to others, and the multiplier effect goes to work.

With these employees, management's role is to:

- Negotiate solid goals
- Give employees the authority to get the job done
- Ask for the feedback that you need for information and guidance
- Move out of the way and make the dream happen

Making the dream the boss and the focus of combined, orchestrated accomplishments can lead to the ultimate team-zone, where excitement and camaraderie override individual concerns. If you strive for this level, please remember to shape monetary gains as team, not individual, payoffs.

Comparing Traditional and Emerging Management Skills

A comparison of the old skills that were needed to motivate unmotivated employees and the new skills needed to manage motivated employees is presented in Table 6–1.

In the new set of motivation skills, everyone is valued, a partnership exists among levels, and a collaborative effort is mandated.

Decade One: The Emerging Employee Profile

To scope the organizational game in 2000+ you must deal with the leading-edge images of the current organizational shapers. The core theories of the quality movement, new organizational architectures, and cultural transformations suggest a collage of the future that may contain attributes such as:

- Self-motivation and responsibility

Table 6–1. The great management paradox (pursuing motivation in 2000+).

Traditional Skills	Emerging Skills
Direct people.	Teach self-motivation.
Do things well.	Do great things.
Hold a tight rein.	Sit lightly in the saddle.
Be the expert.	Teach others.
Earn personal respect.	Develop partnerships.
Be logical.	Be intuitive.
Say yes to your ego.	Shape a group ego.
Order the behavior.	Model the behavior.
Be in control.	Enable self-control.
Be responsible.	Build joint accountability.
Emphasize activities.	Emphasize results.
Allow budgets to guide decisions.	Let values guide decisions.
Require conformity.	Encourage creativity.
Follow the chain of command.	Follow the customer.
Be strong.	Empower.
Get with the program.	Challenge the process.
Get compliance.	Encourage commitment.

- Creativity
- Self-initiation of activity
- Flexibility
- Quick learning
- Team tendencies
- An outward (customer) focus
- Broad perspective
- Commitment, but not necessarily sacrificial
- A challenge to existing systems
- Continuous improvement seeking

In the lists of visions, missions, and values of today's progressive organizations, these kinds of attributes are already common. No longer can an organization intelligently adopt the

Marine motto, "All we need is a few good men!" Aside from the obvious sexism and lack of understanding of the future labor pool, this slogan ignores the need for legions of diverse people who understand, value, and are willing to stand tall and talented in the whirlwind of the twenty-first century.

The 2000+ People Pipeline

So who is going to make all this happen in "Decade One," just over the 2000 timeline? The organizational people population will be drawn from the ranks of current younger employees, incoming college graduates, current high school students, and those who have dropped out or stopped out of the education system. They will come from communities representing many different cultures.

Generalizations suggest that our colleges, universities, high schools, and homes are the training and learning grounds for our future workforce. What goes on in our schools and homes? The irony is that our young people are learning some counterproductive things, such as:

• Everyone is entitled to everything. We all get everything, and we all get innumerable chances.

• Trying is enough. As long as you make an attempt, you will pass and move on to the next level.

• Everyone has equal rights. Every award, starting position, nomination, and decision by principals, deans, or other administrators is subject to challenge. Exercising rights is more important than learning to take responsibility, accepting the good with the bad, being resilient, and persevering in the face of bad luck, unfairness, and failed promises.

• Structure, discipline, and clear guidelines are not available.

• Scapegoating is a way out of responsibility. It's not your fault. You are a victim of your circumstances.

• It's not what's right or wrong but what is technically

achievable. Run to daddy, mommy, or someone else who will either talk the administration out of their decision or threaten to sue.

• We live in the age of the feckless family. The above learning creates a new generation of parents. Parents, busy and tired from trying to make it in the 1990s (both are working, maybe not even living together), can't discipline, control, or even provide good, consistent advice to their kids. Different schedules, interests, agendas, and distractions unravel the fabric of even the most well-intentioned child raisers.

The "Organizational Need—People Pipeline" Paradox

Even if you think that we have exaggerated the problem, we believe that you will admit that the people products of our society, schools, and families are different from earlier ones. Our young people rightfully expect to be treated fairly. But they have been allowed to become great manipulative managers. Conflict arises when they encounter the realities faced by hard-driving organizations fighting fierce competition through a crusader mission that can't wait for scapegoat artists, weenies, moral wimps, and wafflers. Get with the program or wave bye-bye!

Conversely, this people pipeline can also be a marvelous resource. The ability to challenge the old paradigms, see the idiocy in the way things are, and strive to find a new niche is a potential source of power. But the frailties of immaturity, blame shifting, self-absorption, and the need to be entertained instantly and constantly will tax even the expert motivators. The old joke may take on new meaning and urgency—"The behavior and morale around here is so bad we call our company The Whinery!"

Adding It Up

Three different skills are needed to manage a diversely motivated workforce. Managers must learn how to motivate externally those who need this, develop self-motivation in those who want it, and manage those who are already self-motivated. As empowerment spreads, developing self-motivation and managing motivated people will become more and more important in the new millennium.

The art of dealing with motivated employees is not easy. The type of employee is changing. But the rewards are great. Allowing self-motivated people the freedom to decide unleashes great sources of energy in them while freeing your time for dream making and goal setting. Just remember to set up a reporting structure that will keep you in touch with what they do and to provide the needed feedback. Ask for what you want!

Action Exercise 6-1

1. What is the most common frustration that you face? Is it goal blockage or goal conflict?

2. How could you solve it?

3. Name five potential motivators that you might try.

   1. _____

   2. _____

   3. _____

   4. _____

   5. _____

4. How comfortable are you giving up part of your power?

5. What training might you take to enhance your delegation skills?

6. When it comes to managing motivated people, what skills are your strongest? Weakest?

Action Exercise 6–2

The hope of promotion can be a motivating factor. But these days you may be waiting for Godot at the promotion window, following a false prophet/profit!

As a reality check, take out your company's succession planning roster from five years ago and find out where everyone is today! After you get over your elation or depression, think about what you can learn from the differences as they pertain to your future.

7

Etching the Clarity

*"Practice straight expectations, not management
by mind-reading!"*

Getting things straight, up-front, and on-line, in any situation,
establishes a baseline for successful doing. "Communication
failure" is often the result of a lack of clarity, not of poor word
choices. Effective organizational communications isn't memos,
handbooks, or electronic transmissions but an accurate, common understanding.

At one time or another, poor communication has been
blamed for most of the world's ills. Attributing disasters to poor
communication is usually prefaced by something like, "You
know, 90 percent of the problems on earth are caused by a lack
of communication!" While there is no clear way to authenticate
statements like this, we know intuitively that the statement has
merit. Communication is the roadbed, the forcefield, the linking
verb in any organization.

As the information highway makes unheard-of types and
amounts of information available, the trick becomes knowing
how to get the information you need and how to organize and
process the data.

In organizations, the process of communication takes one
of three forms (for the moment, we will set aside intuitive or
subconscious communication):

1. Verbal (telephone)
2. Written (letters, memos, policies and procedures, faxes, E-mail)
3. Face-to-face

Successful communication in each of these mediums requires some preparation, specific skills, and a "tuning in." Telephone conversations call for close attention to vocal cues, since the other party can't see you to interpret body language and facial expressions. Written communications are enduring and must be constructed carefully to avoid a long-lasting misperception. Face-to-face communications are the most complex. The good news is that the receiver can interpret several different clues at the same time to construct and interpret your meaning. The bad news is that the receiver has access to your many subtle signals at the same time to construct and interpret the meaning.

Communication B.C. (Before Competition)

The nature of feedback has changed dramatically in recent years. Way back in B.C. times (Before Competition), most internal communications were bland, restricted, third-person (for example, "The management has decided . . .), and controlled through a biased, "need-to-know" distribution. Why should anyone but the top staff need to know where the organization is going? Even the mission and goals of the enterprise were often kept from the troops. "Management by mind reading" was developed into an art form![1]

Communication A.D. (After Deming)

When fierce competition arrived in the late 1970s and early 1980s, organizations drowning in red ink reached what psychol-

1. For a more thorough explanation of management by mind reading, see: Ken Matejka, *Why This Horse Won't Drink: How to Win and Keep Employee Commitment!* (New York: AMACOM, 1991).

ogists call a "teachable moment." An important communication lesson learned from Dr. W. Edwards Deming's quality movement was that flawed, partial, ambiguous communications irritate rather than motivate. Now, in Organizations A.D. (After Deming), people at all levels are more conscious of their communication effort. Clear communications are important in managing strategic issues, in face-to-face and written transmissions from executives to supervisors, from marketing to finance, from computer to computer, or from fax to fax. A shared vision and empowerment have directly led people to now want and expect "full disclosure."

The Twelve Facets of Fertile Feedback

The changing expectations of the workforce regarding the right to receive frequent, meaningful feedback about everything and the responsibility of managers to provide that feedback skillfully set up a new dynamic.

People want and now expect fast, straight, timely feedforward and feedback. When information becomes the "gold" of the twenty-first century, it will be even more important to try to hone your communication skills so that, no matter what the chosen medium, you can provide feedback that is:

1. Private
2. Expected
3. Results-oriented
4. Frequent
5. Optimistic
6. Relevant
7. Mission-driven
8. Assertive
9. Need-based
10. Constructive
11. Educational
12. Specific

We have arranged these twelve attributes so that they spell out the word *PERFORMANCES!* While this may seem a little corny, we hope that this will make it easier for you to remember the premises of great feedback. When practiced properly, these twelve attributes can help to clean up lots of clogged communications.

Establishing Straight Expectations

Telling people exactly what you expect from them is a tough assignment. It's natural to be a little cautious, a little apprehensive, a little mystical, a little secretive. But whatever you say unclearly or don't say at all becomes a potential minefield for you and the employees. The differences among thoughts, actions, and words led Marriott Corporation to adopt the slogan "People don't do what you expect, they do what you inspect."

Privately held expectations are a trap for both parties. Expecting an employee to act a certain way without clearly telling her is management by mind-reading! No matter how noble your intentions, when even your best employee is forced to survive by reading your mind, you have set the stage for failure. Just remember, we're all the same, only different. Nobody else thinks, understands, decides, and reacts exactly like you. Keep in mind that:

• Employees reject hidden messages (sandwiched-in mixed meanings and obscure metaphors). People hear what they choose and suspect the sender.

• Employees reject unclear messages. If it's not meaningful, they block it or invest greatly in interpretive gossip.

• Employees reject inconsistent messages. Such messages either cancel each other out or give the employee a best choice.

• Employees reject silent expectations. They really can't read your mind, but the nonverbal cues you send make them apprehensive.

Do your best to deliver "straight expectations." As a sophisticated manager, you should:

- Get clear about what you want
- Ask for what you want
- Show the employee how he or she will benefit
- Relate the request to performance, not to your personal biases. (When you know that your wants are personal biases, it's legitimate to have them. Just own up to it and label them for what they are.)
- Expect only what you have clearly requested

If you don't have the courage to ask for what you want, perhaps you don't deserve to get it. The results are better when you practice "straight expectations," not "management by mind reading!" There is a hot side to straight expectations. When you ask for things genuinely and straight up, people are more likely to respond.

Getting Straight With Yourself

You can't expect people to know what you want unless you tell them. However, lots of people aren't at all clear about what they want, what's bothering them, or where they want to go next. You are your own best resource for describing your own thoughts, feelings, and needs. Your internal processor is working full time sorting out what is happening to you. The output is a collection of choices, decisions about all that is going on, and it shows up as an internal list. It is this simple:

1. What do you want?
2. What are you doing?
3. How is it working?
4. What is your plan—if what you've been doing isn't working or takes too much work?

Life and relationships would be easy if people could know what they need, know where that is and whom to go to, and have the ability to ask, and ask with power. It doesn't work that way because we have a hundred ways to: keep on noodling in our heads; distract ourselves with side issues; talk ourselves out of what we want; exaggerate the weakness or situation of the other person and withhold the powerful demand; and soften it, distort it, aim it at the wrong person, or deflect it into a side issue.

Since you are your own best source for what you need, why don't you know more about that? Our early training and experience often set us up to please others, avoid risk, suffer in silence, go along, and be a good person, not rock the boat or the program. Most people, in fact, really don't know what they want. There are, however, ways to get at it:

1. Listen to your internal chatter. What are you muttering to yourself? Say that out loud when you are alone, and find some new data.

2. Where is the pain? Feel the tension in your muscles—pain in the neck (picture who that is); spasm in the leg (whom do you want to kick?); pain in the eyes (what don't you want to see?). Shoulder pain may reflect a feeling of carrying a burden or anger. Let your muscles talk back to you and find out what you need.

3. Go with the gut. Intuition seats itself often in the abdominal area. The flicks of excitement, fear, or tension may have a message for you. Tune in and listen to your inner messages. Decisions that don't feel right in the gut are often, later, found to be very wrong. Make a gut check a regular safety item.

4. Shut down the external buzz, the TV, the sound system, the machinery. Listen to the total picture on your own. If you know how, go back to the silent time for inner focus (e.g., meditation).

5. If you have been building a personal dream as we suggest in Chapter 4, that is a great place to check out what you want and what is missing in your life.

Our irrationalities, distortions, and blind spots keep even the clearest needs and wants from coming into focus. Human beings naturally distort information due to biases (subjective "learnings"), blind spots (things that we cannot see about ourselves), and blank spots (missing pieces of data or experience). Check out your personal system for these common pollutors of your success climate.

• *Hidden biases.* A bias is a prejudice (pre-judgment) or a preference. Biases are subjective and, as such, are potential obstacles to clear communication. When we allow biases to impinge on the rights, freedoms, or opportunities of other people, the biases become unfair and distasteful. Prejudices can cost your organization lost opportunities, efficiencies, sales, or profits. In organizational settings, biases can be related to jobs (for example, seeing Human Resources as a "soft" function) or how the jobs get done (choosing a "style" over actual performance or a preferred manner of dress). Biases are filters that color the way we view the world.

Sometimes you can take the light, humorous approach to dealing with biases. One potential strategy is to use the sentence: "That's what _____ tend to say!" For example, when a finance manager is laying financial biases on the group as the answer to the organization's problems, you could announce gently, with a smile, "That's what finance people tend to say!" This light touch can be truly effective.

• *Blind spots.* Blind spots are things about ourselves that we are not aware of but that others readily see. Caution: Blind spots can be hazardous to your career! Blind spots can operate in many spheres. Consider:

- The dog owner who isn't aware of the noise problem
- The considerate person who once behind the wheel of a car becomes a reckless, aggressive driver and a menace
- A mechanic with four disassembled cars in his yard who is unaware of the "sight pollution" problem he is causing for his neighbors
- The "slob" at work, unaware of the food in his moustache, the stains on his tie, his bad breath, or his unkempt hair

- The engineer who doesn't perceive his lack of appreciation for the problems faced by the marketing department

- *Blank spots.* Sometimes, the barrier is neither prejudice nor unseen frailties but a black hole—a lack of understanding, education, or experience that leaves the person clueless on the subject. More and more, learning is becoming less permanent, and skills must be refurbished or you are out of touch. There are still a few managers who proudly exclaim that they know nothing about computers and refuse to learn. This pride in ignorance is tragic and laughable. Getting straight with yourself is tough work, but the rewards are immense.

Getting Straight With Others

Getting clear and straight with yourself is the first step to getting straight with others.

People act and react according to their perceptions. In many ways, it doesn't matter whether you are right, just how you or your views are perceived. Suppose that you are marching in a parade and you are on your left foot when others are on their right foot. Maybe you are correct, but it doesn't matter, does it? The goal is for the entire band to be in step. What is more expedient—for you to switch or for everyone else to switch? This is neither a plea for conformity or an "atta girl" for taking the road less traveled. It is a plea to see what is there as a starting point.

Total Listening Concentration

The best way to show respect to another human being is to be willing to hear what he or she has to say—to give the person some TLC! There is an old saying that people don't care what you know until they know that you care! A great way to learn while showing your respect is to seriously study and practice Total Listening Concentration (TLC). TLC requires you to focus all of your attention on the other person and to try as intently as possible to understand what he is trying to tell you.

TLC requires that you:

• *Don't talk!* Shut up and learn. Your silence surfaces more truth. You can't learn what the other person thinks while you are talking. Do not lead the discussion. Do not interrupt. Learn what the speaker wants you to learn. As Archie Bunker used to say, "Stifle yourself!"

• *Prepare yourself to listen!* Clear your mind. Clear your workspace. And clear your hands. No calls! No paper shuffling. Focus on what the speaker is saying. Pretend there will be a test later! (There usually is, in the speaker's mind.)

• *Be aware of your nonverbal messages!* Pay attention to body language and facial expressions—the speaker's and yours. Pay attention to the gaps, the energy level, the positivity ratio. (This is a trick item. Although your nonverbal behavior must be in sync with your verbal message, if you were truly concentrating, the appropriate body language would happen automatically. When you are faking concern, the wrong body language gets exhibited.)

Just in case, try not to let your opinions show.

• *Get rid of any distractions!* Shut the door. Don't answer the phone. Close the window. Take your watch off, and place it in your desk. Don't tap your fingers or foot.

• *Show respect!* Pretend you are listening to Plato. Show a genuine interest in the speaker's thoughts and opinions.

• *Paraphrase to check for meaning transfer.* When there is silence, let it be for a while. Be patient. If you feel the person needs help, rephrase what you heard her saying. Ask for clarification!

Types of Impoverished Listeners

Most managers are not good listeners. They don't treasure the skill enough to practice it. When you watch someone pretending to listen, you see a caricature—a poor imitation. Most insincere listeners can be grouped into one of five types.

1. *The Fidgeter*—shows disinterest through body language and thinks that listening is a huge imposition

2. *The Type A Listener*—is so intent on being a good listener that he intimidates others with his intensity
3. *The Arrogant Genius*—is deaf to most of what is said because he or she already has the solution to the problem, even if that solution ignores the needs and feelings of the others
4. *The Nodder*—always appears to agree with whomever is speaking because he or she gives continual affirmative nods of the head while listening
5. *The Pseudo-Listener*—manages to listen halfheartedly, misinterpreting and slightly distorting the message being sent

Getting Straight Within Your System: Culture Coping

Every organization has a culture, a fairly stable, unwritten rulebook and a way of doing things. To be successful, you must be able to operate adeptly within the confines of your system. Learn as much as you can about how your organization works, what is acceptable, what is taboo. Many organizations fit into one of the following four culture categories.

1. *The Commonsense Culture.* This culture is tough on employees. Advice to use "common sense" comes from those steeped in the culture. The trouble with common sense is that it is not very common, seldom makes sense, and usually turns into non-sense! For example, it is "common sense" to get rid of disruptive employees so that they don't infect the rest of the workforce. The problem is that often the employee is simply transferred and becomes someone else's problem. If the transfer is to a better climate, then you have actually rewarded the employee—but then again, you already knew that; it's common sense! To communicate in this culture you must frame everything in "common-sense" terms, whether it's appropriate or not. In fact, if you can out-common-sense everyone else, your idea wins.

2. *The "Culture Culprit" Culture.* This culture, driven by the "cult of doing more with less," is the buckle-tightening, budget-slashing, competition-crushing climate that is responsible for the worsening of family life and the decline of leisure among the management ranks through "culture culprit" programs. An example is the "Super Saver" airline ticket which entices companies, by direct order or not-so-subtle implication, to force employees traveling to distant locations to stay over on Saturday night. The Saturday Night Special was created in the U.S. Airlines Halls of Wisdom to promote travel over the weekend. Whatever the initial motive, it has become a fixture in pricing. Savings are at least 50 percent of regular fares. The employee's lost weekend is a gift to the employer, cutting costs and carving out extra time at the task. The corporate keepers call it, not sacrifice, but dedication, loyalty, or, in the new lexicon, "buy-in to our vision!" Forget family outings and interactions. How can you complain? Church services are offered all day Sunday in the basement of O'Hare Field in Chicago. This inadvertent consequence is not the tail wagging the dog but the tail wagging the whole zoo. Adding insult to injury, organizations often insist that frequent flyer miles be used for organizational business trips. Alas, in the culture culprit culture, one of the few benefits that accrue from spending huge chunks of your life in stale, stuffed planes and snarled airports has been confiscated. No longer can you take someone you want to a place you want to go to in exchange for the lost time and opportunities. To communicate effectively in this culture, just relate everything to cost savings and "can-do buy-in," regardless of the impact on people.

3. *The Cowboy Culture.* Rope 'em, brand 'em, herd 'em! This organizational emulation of the Old West is a nasty place. The cultural motto is "shoot first, ask questions later." Ready, fire, aim! Quick-draw contests between employees are everyday entertainment. Only the fastest guns survive. To communicate in this culture, you had better be able to talk fast, get to the point, and then head for the hills before they find out who that masked man was.

4. *The Caring Culture.* This culture respects people's opinions, ideas, skills, and feelings. Communicating effectively in

this culture is a piece of cake, since the organization values warmth, closeness, intensity, and caring! If you have ever worked in this climate, you will always remember it and want it to last.

Show What You Know

The lights are on. The cameras are rolling. There are 10,000 anxious spectators in the organization. The teleconference is being beamed worldwide. The manager steps to the microphone to speak to the employees about motivation. She'd better be prepared. She'd better be skilled. She'd better be motivated! After her presentation, the communications analysts will critique and rerun the key segments of her talk, in slow motion if needed, to dissect word, intonation, facial expression, and body language. Sound scary? If athletes have to perform under this kind of close scrutiny, why shouldn't managers? No manager should ask an employee to perform a behavioral task that the manager isn't willing to demonstrate expertly in front of a crowd of 50,000 people and glaring TV cameras.

Showing is modeling the desired behavior. The manager becomes the actor, demonstrating the desired behavior. In reality, there is a huge difference between knowing and showing. For example, you can memorize and remember five motivational theories (stowing), learn to apply them (knowing), and be able to integrate them (growing), but the true leadership depends on whether you can demonstrate the knowledge (showing). Talking about motivation isn't as important as being motivated. Can you lead when it is needed? Can you give a great speech, or just talk about giving one? Can you communicate through your behavior? Can you walk the talk? When it comes to communication, you don't really know it unless you can show it!

Bestow What You Know

To communicate effectively in the new millennium, you will have to be a teacher. There can be little doubt that the organizational changes currently in place and on the horizon will lead to the inevitable conclusion that the primary skill of managing in the twenty-first century will be to teach! Macho management is out; mentoring is in! Terrorizing is out; teaching is in! Showing off is out; showing how is in! Condescension is out; collaborative learning is in!

The good news is: It's about time. Have you noticed how few workers are bemoaning the demise of the old management styles? The bad news is: Change can be tough on all of us. The manager will be a teacher of motivated employees, and the ability to develop fully diverse employees will be increasingly critical to organizational success.

The leader will no longer be the sage, seer, guru, or master but will instead be the navigator, helper, guide, or colleague. And for good reason. Active collaborative learning is more effective in most cases. Adults learn best by asking questions. Employee involvement is critical to optimum learning.

Finally, it's time to give something back! Someone showed you how; now it's your turn. The manager must become a teacher and share the understanding with others. There is no greater professional responsibility and personal satisfaction than to give back what someone else has given to you by helping others to see what you see and know what you know. You must become a teacher of teachers.

Collaborative learning is working together, side-by-side, student and guide. To be a great collaborative teacher, you must be:

- Passionate enough to attract others
- Knowledgeable enough to be an expert
- Experienced enough to handle the unexpected
- Secure enough not to feel threatened by any question
- Insightful enough to make the difficult simple
- Enthusiastic enough to communicate in provocative and evocative ways
- Capable enough to meld form and function into one attractive whole
- Skilled enough to inspire a lifelong quest for learning

The Clarity Connection

When straight and candid, skilled and caring, the communication link makes dream shaping, dream-team creating, and culture changing possible! Practice straight communications—etch the clarity.

Action Exercise 7–1

Think of five ways that you might be able to improve communication with some members of your diverse workforce.

1. _____

_____

2. _____

_____

3. _____

_____

4. _____

_____

5. _____

_____

Action Exercise 7–2

Pick out a peer or employee on whom to practice your listening skills. Invite the person into your office, close the door, take the phone off the hook, and ask some pertinent questions relating to work. Listen closely, clarify when needed, and try to feed back your understanding of what the person is trying to tell you. Remember, you are trying to understand, as closely as possible, what this person is trying to say. Wipe out your opinions, and try total listening concentration!

Action Exercise 7-3

Organizational culture determines the corporate communication style. The following statements are indicators of the organizational communication patterns.

Indicate the extent to which these statements describe your organization's culture.

1	2	3	4	5
Strongly Agree	**Agree**	**Not Sure**	**Disagree**	**Strongly Disagree**

_____ 1. An honest open-door policy is the exception where you work.

_____ 2. Looking busy is more important than being busy.

_____ 3. Getting it done fast is more important than getting it right.

_____ 4. Employee suggestions are not taken seriously.

_____ 5. You need an appointment to see your boss.

_____ 6. Employees are treated like family.

_____ 7. Legendary organizational heroes are discussed.

_____ 8. One of the organizational mottos is "A clean desk is a happy desk!"

_____ 9. Safety is more important than production.

_____ 10. Quality is more important than quantity.

_____ 11. The way meetings are conducted, they are a waste of time.

_____ 12. This used to be an enjoyable place to work.

_____ 13. It's okay to laugh and have fun as long as you produce.

_____ 14. Everyone is an equal part of the team.

_____ 15. Conflicts are swept under the table.

Three

Your Personal Readiness Manual

Here is another paradox: Does this book offer a survival manual or a framework for prevailing in the organization? The answer is yes. Focusing on the word "prevail" shifts the paradigm and says that survival is not enough. We want you to join the battle as full partners, knowing that the fun is, indeed, in the going! The victories and defeats are simply more learning, more growing, and . . . more to come. Next?

Realizing Your Potential and Expanding the Possibilities

The life paths and career tracks you learned about when you were a child don't really exist anymore. You, your kids, and even your grandkids will be dismayed to find how hard it is to find a "real job" after college graduation. The default solution: Go for a degree, another degree, a higher degree. Often, the job opportunities don't increase even then. Our advice in the mid-1980s about this job thing would have been to learn how to get in, stay in, and move up by hard work, being visible, and keeping your nose clean!

That's still not bad advice. But getting in and staying in are now more difficult. Organizations are flatter, more fluid, and more flexible. You, as a component, are a movable part. Our new advice has two phases. First, find a job (always a good start), make a job (start your own business), or reinvent your job (if dropped, ask to start a subbusiness in the company and see if you can make it go). Then, find a job (here we go again); be valuable quickly; become fully inserted and committed, quickly; and be ready to move (whether your choice or theirs). Be alive and well in transition; outside and looking in can be a fascinating learning experience. Last, create your own imagery to picture yourself (e.g., as a high-performance SWAT team, a mobile task force, a rapid deployment unit, a laser-guided heat-seeking missile).

The point is that settling in and settling down in your new job or job assignment needs to happen on "quick time." Be ready and on-line right now. It isn't even old-fashioned to be eager (if you are still into being "cool," your learning is still at a historic, basic level). You must be the nomad, the lifelong "temp," the free-floating particle. "Finding a job" is a permanent condition in the Age of 2000+. If you should be lucky enough to sign on for what turns out to be thirty years, then the advice in this book will help keep you valued and moving inside your system. Being at "battle-ready" will keep you sharp, focused, and high-performing. Work from a position of "lifelong learner." Learn the technology; learn about leadership and organizations; learn about people; learn about yourself as the core of people learning; learn how to manage yourself through a whirlwind of emotions without falling into the permanent abyss of bitterness, anger, and discontent. The four chapters in this section will help you in finding a job, working a job, and being ready for the next job challenge. We hope to expand your personal new possibilities.

Specifically, we present strategies to enhance your career, manage the tough new people problems, cope with the most baffling new types of problem people, positively assist yourself and your organization, and help you prevail when you are the recipient (and victim) of these grand new organizational changes.

8

Enhancing Your Advancement and Advancing Your Enhancement

"We aren't sure what's wrong with your organization, but we will know more right after the autopsy."

The old straight-up career ladder is dead. Besides, most of the rungs are now gone. Hierarchy is out. The team is more important than the star. Personal and corporate improvement is continuous. Process is as important as results. Empowerment determines managerial success. Employees support customers. Managers support employees. It is indeed a global, connected, interdependent world.[1]

Promotion in the future will be more like mountain climbing—choosing the right route, making adjustments dictated by the environment, fostering a team support effort, and sometimes

---

1. The first two paragraphs and all of the material on choosing advancement, including the ten pointers, were excerpted from Dick Dunsing and Ken Matejka, "Enhancing Your Advancement in the 1990s," *Management Decision*, 31, no. 1 (1993): 127–133.

going sideways or down in order to get up eventually. A successful climb requires preparation, planning, and conditioning. As you probably know, our competitive world has been turned upside down, and these changes affect strategies for getting promoted. The art of advancement is a whole new ballgame. Getting promoted will never again be the same. The path to the top is full of a bunch of new twists and turns.

Choosing Advancement

Pursuing a promotion is one of those good news-bad news stories. The bad news is that opportunities are shrinking. While most people feel that they deserve to be promoted, corporate downsizing has reduced the number of levels and positions available. The good news is that not everyone wants a promotion. Furthermore, in new, developing, bottom-up organizations, *to enhance is not necessarily to advance!* People may be comfortable in their current jobs and may not want the change in activities and/or the added responsibilities that advancement brings. Some people make a valid, conscious choice not to seek advancement. It is okay not to seek a promotion! In fact, staying in your current position may be the wise choice. Reaching for the brass ring has its perils, as well as its rewards. The formula for getting promoted has always been part merit, part loyalty, part conformity, part creativity, and part favoritism, along with a generous portion of luck. But if promotion is what you truly desire, we provide ten "promotion pointers" for enhancing your advancement in the twenty-first century.

The New Path to Promotion

1. *Performance.* In the old, autocratic, pyramidal organizations, you could easily hide in the comfort of your functional area. While being the best accountant still helps when the promotion decisions are being made, it is not enough anymore. Skills in leading, listening, managing change, building alliances, brainstorming, developing teams, sculpting commitment, developing creativity, and enhancing quality through consensus have

become more significant factors in the promotion equation. Coordination is replacing cooptation. Collaboration skills are taking the place of competitive abilities. Performance now means function skills and human expertise.

2. *Presence.* The old style was to stand out. But as the old Japanese proverb says, the nail that stands up gets hammered down. The new style is not so much to blend in as to be the blender. Blending requires being a catalyst, facilitator, and coach, rather than the driving force. If your people skills work well, the team will in fact drive your success. You will stand out through the reflected success. For you to get promoted, your group's achievements (and therefore your leadership) must get noticed. Perceptions of your ability to bring the team together to accomplish a common goal are critical to your promotional potential. The shift that is occurring in this variable is in how you get noticed (as leader of a great team) and in who gets the credit (the team and therefore you). Sharing the responsibility and credit with team members is gaining in popularity. Do not be phony, but do spread the credit around. Take the most sincere and least vulgar route to visibility. Work the paradox well: Nobody likes a show-off, but out of sight means out of mind! Visibility means that you take and share honest credit for your group's achievements and professionally let others know about your work as team leader. Leaders must walk a fine line between conceit and humility, individual contribution and team success. You can brag about your team, but not about yourself. Make sure the team gets attention for its achievements, and recognition of yours will follow. Once you are convinced that your team's ideas have rightfully been attributed, forget about it and move on to the next challenge.

3. *Priorities.* Not long ago, rules dominated behavior. In the future, values will dominate rules. Every organization has, or will have, an expensively developed list of values and guiding principles. What will your organization stress? Confronting or smoothing? Individual or group values? Loyalty or honesty? Quantity or quality? Conformity or creativity? Knowing the value system within your organization and acting accordingly will be critical to your success. When push comes to shove, re-

wards will go to those people who act in ways consistent with the company's values.

4. *Problem solving.* The group is becoming the preferred unit for problem solving. A sure way to separate yourself or your group from your peers is to bring solutions, not problems, to your superiors. We all have enough problems. None of us wants more work, especially when it was not our idea. Find out what is stifling your own productivity and your boss's productivity, and develop creative solutions. Most bosses love subordinates with solutions. Involve the team so that it can practice problem-solving skills. If nothing else, the boss can either brag about the team or pretend the idea was hers. Openly sharing your ideas may create a climate in which all workers can share. To ensure team (and your) credit, see pointer 2.

5. *Persuasion.* Politics is out (or at least it is and will become less blatant), and persuasion is in. Whether you like it or not, you must influence the decision makers in your shop. You do not have to butter people up, but you do have to be sophisticated about the formal and informal lines of communication. Some people have more influence than others. Be yourself, but do not be naïve about the coalitions being formed to gain acceptance of people and ideas. The days are gone when doing your job like a good little Indian and minding your own business could get you promoted. Today, isolation is a do-it-yourself hangman's kit. Use your persuasive abilities to get your group the resources it needs.

6. *Power.* Hierarchical power is out. Empowerment is in. Power is often perceived negatively as coercion, dishonesty, and taking advantage of others. But there is much more to power. Power is a necessary part of being a manager. If you have no power, you cannot get your subordinates what they need to do their job well. Similarly, if you are going to get the correct ideas accepted, you will need to be able to influence the important players. Build respect with your proficiency, position, and personality. Learn the art of persuasion. Build your potential for advancement. Power has many faces—learn to use all of them! But remember, the change lately has been to move away from doing things for the sake of making an impact (power motive)

and toward giving ownership of tasks to your people so that they can meet an inner standard of excellence (the achievement motive).

7. *Participation.* Participation is becoming an increasingly critical process in most competitive organizations. Do not overlook the importance of continually getting input and genuine involvement from your associates. First, employees with ownership in problems and issues become more committed. Second, if you continue to make all the decisions, you squash development in two ways: You will become too valuable in your current position to be promoted, and you will keep your people mentally undernourished and overly dependent. Help your people to grow and develop. Give those who want it more input, more interaction, and more responsibility. Free yourself to be promoted or enhanced while empowering your people.

8. *Presentation.* To advance in tomorrow's world, you will need to be able to present yourself and your ideas convincingly, both in writing and verbally. Have you noticed how it has become impossible for a presidential candidate to be elected if he is not able to present himself credibly on television? Organizations are not far behind. Whether you like it or not, you must appear to be at ease and in command in front of other people. Presentation skills will become even more critical as individuals and groups interact at greater distances through teleconferencing and whatever channels tomorrow's technology brings.

9. *Passion.* Passionate people with dreams attract followers. When you seem uninterested, why should others get excited? Watch the powerful people you know, and you will see simple, clear ideas championed by enthusiastic leaders. Passion is lacking in many organizations, which is one key reason they are mediocre. The greatest contribution you can make to an organization is to help people believe and act as if it is *their* organization. Passion, fortunately, is contagious—and passionate teams stand out.

10. *People.* Treat your associates as if they were customers. Better yet, pretend that you have to be reelected by your people at the end of each year. Will they vote you in or out? People

decide who gets promoted. People make a boss look good by their performances. People are the end, not the means of production!

Managing your career is a continuous, lifelong procedure. If moving up that organizational ladder is your goal, paying attention to the ten variables we have just discussed should help. The recent and continuing changes in how organizations work have made the climb up the organizational ladder a new, exciting, crooked journey. For this ascent, you will need a new kind of cross-training in the many new skills emerging and being emphasized. Maintain your anchor in your specialty, but broaden your knowledge of anything and everything your organization does. Change is the constant, and lifelong learning is the tool! Make your shop the best there ever was, and a path to your future personal success will be revealed!

Choosing Enhancement

If dropping in and out of organizations is the paradigm for the future, one metaphor for the organization dweller is the desert camel driver who learns to load up, gear up for the long haul, be ready for anything, know where his oasis is.

Enhancement: The Alternative to Advancement

If you haven't yet started watering your camel, think about this. There is a huge Catch-22 here. You will most likely be an organization dweller (we regard this as good news; we need good people like you to be part of the 2000+ organization refitting team). The catch is that the promotion stuff is dead, dying, or only temporary. Why do we say "temporary"? Today's big promotion and attendant salary mark you as a big cost-saving item to the next cutback consultant ("Oh, look, there goes a big one now. Ready, aim, fired.")

Only "enhanced" managers and professionals will make it in tomorrow's organization. You have to think in terms of value added—to yourself and to any system with which you catch on. This means that you have to keep developing a wider range of technical, managerial, and leadership skills. These skills have real power only when they are wrapped in a human being who is deeply committed to understanding what makes people effective and worthwhile in a kaleidoscopic world.

The sages of leadership say that organizations can't prosper without loyal people who are committed to the grand venture. While this approach has great merit, it may be the wrong focus at times. The right focus may be what loyalty and commitment do for *those who give them.* Employees, managers, and the rest must experience intense commitment and deep loyalty to become fully alive. Learning to be committed and to nurture the natural desire to be loyal to something is a pathway to personal growth. Growing in 2000+ will require us to learn how to be:

- *Committed*—even though key people throughout don't seem to be committed.

- *Loyal*—in spite of the disloyalty that seems rampant in the system.

- *Trusting*—a gift for you. Protect yourself from the dishonest and the self-serving. That, however, is no reason not to trust. Trusting behavior is healthy for you. Distrusting eats at your soul.

- *Community builders*—despite the existence of key players with histories of nasty jealousies and raw corporate competitiveness. The yearning for community is deep and real to most people around you. Want it, and work for it. The growing legions of people who came from dysfunctional families and who had less-than-nurturing childhoods will, if encouraged, leap at the chance for finding family-like caring in the workplace.

In addition, give space and power to others. Even though the reward systems isolate people and encourage the self-serving act, you have to give it away and be open to receiving from others.

- *Giving to the organization*—even though the organization

is, in fact, often undeserving and shallow and seems to be ready to abandon you to the highest corporate raider. Trust but verify; cut the cards! You don't have a choice.

Being a Source of Leadership

Want to be a leader? Lots of people do. Many do not. Many more would feel better about leadership if we could explain it, teach it, reward it. At its worst, leadership is a charismatic shaman pitching a personal vision relentlessly and capturing all in front of it. This definition reserves leadership for the lead horse on a trail ride (the only one, so they say, for whom there is a change of scenery). At its most egalitarian, leadership is a broad-based, all-for-one environment where everyone picks up the ball and runs with it, when and where needed.

There are two major dimensions of leadership. The first is the focus on outcomes—of dreams, missions, strategy, or plans. The second is the dynamic process of people engaging their energies and talents together. We are much better in designing hard-nosed plans for success than we are in getting all the noses pointed in the right direction and not out of joint. The pace of events, the shifting responsibilities, and the lack of nurturing in the environment have brought a set of needs to the leadership function that can be pushed forward from anywhere in the organization. Being a channel of leadership, regardless of rank or function, is the level of enhancement you need.

New Leadership Components

Healing

There is a lot of pain, other people's and our own, to be healed—divisions, conflicts, old hurts, losses, missed opportunities. Healing in the traditional organization looks like this:

- The "suck it up and play on" school
- The "you have to learn to play with pain" heavies
- The "if you can't stand the heat" cliché lovers

- The wildly sympathetic, "no one said it would be easy" crowd
- The "I told you so" bunch

Organizations are in need of healers. Hard play makes for wild success and inevitable hurts and setbacks. "Atta boys/girls" go a long way. So does taking the time to hear people out and being empathetic. People who are breaking their backs for you want to know that you care when they skin their knees. When you convince yourself that you are too busy to stop and encourage "the hurting people," you send messages that cut commitment for years to come. And fake attention won't do it. It enhances you to care and heal. You will learn how.

The heavy need for healing, however, is between the warring parties. Individuals in deep conflict can be brought together. There is a skill set to learn that makes that possible. Departments and units can be healed. Customer service people who get beat up by irate customers need more than an encouraging word to keep themselves sound and solid.

Dreaming

Dreaming is the source of inspiration and a vibrant future. Believe it or not, vision making is not a linear process. Asking the planning department to write a vision is like asking an atheist to lead the prayer group. Visions of the possible come from the heart, the intuition, the depths. Dreams are the basis for hard goals and solid plans.

Taking Advantage of Rhythms and Cycles

Life is not a straight-line event, and things seldom come out even. In spite of the annual plan and the Boss's stemwinder speech, things go up and go down, and that is the way it is. "So it goes," wrote Kurt Vonnegut. Peak performance is on the crest of a curve, not a permanent state. The bottom of the cycle can be a creative time to take stock, sort out, catch up, and clean up. It is in the bottom-out moment that illuminations occur and the great "Aha!" happens. The dimension for you to develop is the appreciation of rhythms and cycles—that, and how to draw a growth and learning experience from them. The financial people draw only straight-line growth charts. Reality is different; "down times" can be times of great effectiveness—only in other dimensions.

Celebrating

"Up times" on the organizational cycle should always be punctuated by celebration. Celebration is a natural need that is usually subverted and labeled as abnormal by "Executive Row." Celebration should be simple, spontaneous, and planned by those involved. Celebrate success. Don't stop there. Celebrate honest tries, great learnings, new partnerships, births of ideas, and risks well taken, even if modest in results. Celebration allows for people to feel those things everyone says we need to do—be committed, care about what happens, jump in, and be invested. Celebration helps counterpoint the downside. When failure hits, bad news spreads, and you missed the mark, the grieving should begin.

Letting Go

Death and dying are a part of organizations, projects, jobs, and people's careers. Alpha and omega. Birth and death. You can't fill the cup until it has been emptied. Elizabeth Kubler-Ross in her 1964 book, *On Death and Dying,* found a pattern in the way humans handle loss. Working with terminal cancer patients, she saw these five stages:

1. Denial
2. Anger
3. Bargaining or negotiating
4. Grief and withdrawal
5. Acceptance

The paradox is that there is real pain to loss ... of life, of job, or of old paradigms. Bury each with dignity and completeness, and the possibilities open up. Dr. Ross describes the death of a human being as the final stage of growth. From that perspective, loss needs to be seen as a positive fulfillment. In our work with organizations, we see the same needs for working through the loss stages to do the deep work of change. The transference of the grief concept to personal job loss in the organization is immediate: the loss of job, of being relocated, of being the loser in a promotion, of a cut in salary or status. The steps are the same:

Denial:	"I can't believe they did that." (Words describe reality. It did, in fact, happen.)
Anger:	"Now I believe you and I am incensed!" (Overtly or in subtle sabotage, this stage is worked long after the need for healthy processing.)
Bargaining/ negotiating:	"I'll take a demotion if I can avoid the transfer, or you can take away my company car to cut expenses." (Please make this "thing" go away.)
Grief and the penetration of pain:	The inner working at all levels takes place, over time, to let go of what was and is nevermore.
Acceptance:	Making available the full resources of the person to work the next event and possibility.

Organizationally, the same steps apply. The mumbling about "I can't believe they did that," the surge of hostility and anger, and the backroom deal-making attempts are clear and normal. Organizations that deliberately bring people together and honestly lay out the facts and listen to the anger, sadness, and loss can help their people get on with it. Leadership is knowing about "letting-go" needs, having the skills that fit, and applying them every time there is a change (loss).

Managing Fear

Fear happens! It's real, often overrated but understated. But the task in the year 2000 is to be the one who handles it personally and takes the time to carry others beyond it.

Hoping Relentlessly

You must be a positive realist. Look for the bright spots. Accentuate the good things. Keep on keeping on. The only other option is to become a drag on yourself and others.

Being a Source of Maturity

Mature people are more effective. It sounds obvious. But then, one person's maturity is another person's stodginess or self-righteousness. If you are to be a prevailer, giving up childhood hangups and being a source of mature thinking, feeling, and acting will bring you into the center of effectiveness. It will alienate those who love the game-playing, manipulative, politicizing stuff of organizations.

Models That Display Maturity

Model:	As a last desperate measure, act like an excruciatingly effective, caring human being. It isn't really that hard.
Model straight talk:	Tell it like it is.
Model being an advocate for the organization:	Tell people we have got to make it work, overcome the naysayers, and get on with it.
Model knowing the power of the unmeasurable:	"If you can't measure it, it must be important." Help people in power avoid destructive decisions they justify by counts.
Model asking the irreverent question:	"Pardon me, sir/madam, but why are we destroying the organization that way?"
Model admitting mistakes and learning from them:	If you want others to own up, learn, and take acceptable risks, you had better be first at bat in the "I did it and I'll fix it"

	department. This goes a long way at home, as well.
Model giving and accepting positive strokes:	Call it praise, acknowledgment, or celebration; when you easily give genuine, caring feedback, you build bridges and relationships. You have to accept them, too, or others won't.
Model being a source of strength:	When the permanent white water is churning, you have to be well grounded, centered, and open to the flow of events.
Model being a source of teamness:	The horizontal organization demands much team integration. Without the historic vertical channels for power dumping and direction giving, leading and managing creates the need for committed connectedness across other people and other teams. You must be a source of positive team attitude.

The Self-Managed Work Team

The self-managed work team is a great idea whose time has still not yet come. It is a great idea, but not on this earth—not in the first quarter of the next century. True self-management can happen only in very narrow contexts where the members are nurtured and fed from outside their system. These efforts should be encouraged and supported. But no large system has the mechanisms needed for free people to make the range of decisions that real self-managing entails. To test this point, ask any member of a supposedly self-managed work team if she can decide *not* to make or do whatever has been assigned to her. What happens if she decides to shift methods, quality levels, or timing on her own? The answer: Someone "higher up" steps in.

There is also the basic fact that not everyone can provide the scope of time perspective and insight to manage complexity well.[2]

The making of teams can be handled by applying a traditional management process: the make-or-buy decision. Teams can be "made" through team building, training, nurturing. This decision implies that the group members, long rewarded for hoarding resources, cloying for credit, and promoting themselves, will somehow change over to the team way. Some people can, indeed, overcome this prior conditioning. But many organizations find that making teams in the ingrained individualistic culture is very expensive and tests the patience of the organizational leadership.

The alternative is to "buy" a team. Assemble a flock from different groups who are naturally inclined to the team way and culture. Or simply hire in the whole group, literally starting from scratch.

The Possibilities

Advancement may come to you; it may even be good for you. However, to count on advancement in the new millennium is to pursue the wrong rabbit. Enhancement of self, professional competence, your own personhood, depth, and perspective are the foundations for prevailing in whatever organizations will become. The motto for the millennium will be "carpe per diem"—seize your daily allowance!

---

2. Elliott Jaques, "In Praise of Hierarchy," *Harvard Business Review* (January-February 1990): 127–133.

Action Exercise 8-1

How are you doing on each of the ten promotional paths?

Jot down one of your strengths and one of your weaknesses for each of the areas.

1. Performance

2. Presence

3. Priorities

4. Problem solving

5. Persuasion

6. Power

7. Participation

8. Presentation

9. Passion

10. People

Action Exercise 8–2
The Enhancement Index

List something that is gone in your life that you have not yet let go of:

Personal:

Job:

Name one person you need to get more clear with right now:
Person:

Message:

List three specific actions you could take to become clearer with the person.

1.

2.

3.

9

The Top Ten People Problems: Different, Deeper, and Distracting

*"Let's face it, managing the
technology is the easy part!"*

In 2000+, organization dwellers—leaders, managers, or non-titled team players—will encounter deeper and different kinds of "people problems." Some of these new problems will come from the nature of organizations and how they function. Some will come from the attitudes, expectations, and behaviors that have evolved in our shrinking, electronically connected planet. Anyone with managerial responsibilities will have to learn to deal with these rapidly changing and quickly growing cultural and organizational people issues. They are merely signs of our times and signposts on the millennium highway.

People Problem 1: Functional Teams With People From Dysfunctional Families

Prison professionals will tell you that you can't rehabilitate people who have never been "habilitated." The tidal wave of commitment to teams faces a similar obstacle—members who are the products of dysfunctional families.

Our culture is producing an increasing number of dysfunctional families. Traditional family structures and "bonded and committed families" are likely to be a minority of family units. In addition to single-parent or divorced-parent families (which are, of course, not necessarily dysfunctional), it is more common now to have an alcoholic family member, someone with a police record, an out-of-wedlock child, or children who are being raised by grandparents. While we honor all people and their struggles, with these diverse family challenges come a wide range of responses from the kids who eventually become the adults who become organizational players. Most of the time, caring and sharing, loving and listening, risking and learning (as ways of being in a deep family relationship) are missing.

Many dysfunctional family members join organizations with their buckets nearly empty. They didn't get the emotional feeding they needed as they grew up. The result is, unfortunately, a characteristic response pattern that is bitter, angry, sad, and fragmented. Teaching "team norms" to people who savor their discontent and enjoy seeing things kept off balance on the job is tough. Open sabotage, subtle subversion, put-downs of others, pettiness, and spitefulness simply continue their childhood life script. It isn't always the lack of training or even senior management commitment that keeps the sharpening of the team from succeeding. It takes just one or two embedded, dysfunctional people to derail an entire unit.

Remember: People in dysfunctional families often attack each other. Some of your employees, raised in these conflict settings, may attack you personally. Just try not to internalize the attack. It's not you; it's just a conditioned response.

Paint team management in three role colors: nurturing parent, applied psychologist, and ring master. The good news is that your playing these three roles may well help the dysfunctional team member to move toward wellness, a marvelous product of top-notch management skill.

People Problem 2: A World (and Organizations) With a Bias Toward Violence

Violence is the solution of choice for many in our global village. Some families, some societies, and some organizations see life as a battle and encourage the violent, "take no prisoners" route. As violence continues to spread throughout society, it is bound to increase in the workplace, as well.

Violence infects the organization at the policy level, too. Downsizing is now a socially acceptable form of organizational violence. The fluid organization in permanent white water is less likely to gain the zeal and loyalty of people. If people see themselves as outsiders, then attacking insiders is more easily justified. Tough corporate decisions mean that good people lose their careers overnight. Without any adequate inner resources and fueled by frustration, some may take the more aggressive route.

In general, men still currently drive the organizational value system. When men talk competitiveness, for many it is just a short jaunt to combativeness. For many men, to be masculine is to be feeling-less and therefore care-less. The "manly" thing to do is to confront aggressively. (This tendency is spreading to women, tired of being the victims.) Violence is acted out in headlines as an assassin guns down the lawyer, the executive, the boss. In the past, fights at work usually consisted of a few punches and some wrestling on the floor before someone broke it up. A black eye, a bloody lip, a few bruises, and back to work. Now, the fight may begin normally, but it is more likely to occur in any setting and to escalate to a knife, handgun, or Uzi. Violence is indeed becoming the frustration solution of choice.

The United States has become an "in your face" culture. Encouraged by assertions of all sorts of personal rights, people feel more aggrieved and more justified in "getting even." Not that violence is new in the workplace. The floor foreman was often the biggest man in the shop, and for good reason: Tough meant respect, and order was established.

Violence will be a continuing reality in 2000+. We haven't got the fortitude to inspect and counter our male-oriented values. Our culture and energies flow more easily toward censoring the sexually explicit than the violently explicit.

There are no easy solutions to violence. We do suggest, however, that you protect yourself at all times—in unlit parking lots and with unenlightened people. Never argue with a crazy person. Finally, it is your duty to remove violent people from the organization in order to protect yourself and your employees.

People Problem 3: The Conflict of Managing Agreement

Managing agreement may be one of the keys to survival. We know what to do but don't do it. Managing agreement is the grand collusion. Jerry Harvey, through his variations on the "Abilene Paradox" theme, has focused on the peculiar approach organization dwellers have to managing agreement. In short, they don't do it. His point is that when major dysfunctions occur in an organization or one of its divisions or units, three things occur:

1. Everyone knows what the problem is.
2. Everyone also knows what has to be done—the solution.
3. No one does anything about it. Everyone all caves in to appease one another and willingly agrees to do something else that no one really wants.[1]

The result is that widespread "agreement" on the problem, as well as the solution, is buried. Misperceiving the will of the others and unwilling to risk possible alienation, everyone avoids confronting the real issue. Thus, there is no focus on positive, productive solutions. Dr. Harvey has a number of interesting ways to describe why rational human beings can engage in such counterproductive behavior. A major reason is our fear of exis-

1. D. Richard Albertson and Jerry B. Harvey, "Neurotic Organizations: Symptoms, Causes and Treatment," *Personnel Journal* (October 1971): 770–776; Jerry B. Harvey, "The Abilene Paradox: The Management of Agreement," *Organizational Dynamics*, 3, no. 1 (Summer 1974): 63–80.

tential alienation by our peers, resulting in ostracism. To say the truth, to say out loud what we really feel and think (which is unknowingly shared by the others), is to take a greater risk (it seems) than it is worth. And the band plays on. The tune is unchanged. Willingly playing off the wrong song sheet, to be sure, but playing together.

Learning how to manage agreement is far better than seeking wise consultants (they cannot usually cough up the collusion any better than the people who run the place) or launching a new management culture approach (e.g., MBO, TQM, or re-engineering). When properly utilized, the core of agreement will throw out what won't work, clear out job misfits, reorder processes that are cumbersome, and get on with it. To manage agreement, however, requires overcoming the needs of the Whiner ("My God, things are actually working here!") and the Doom and Gloom Merchant ("What? Death is not imminent?"). Practicing the skills of straight talk, allowing and protecting risk taking, stroking innovative venturing, and acting on the discoveries in agreement-seeking meetings will change the direction of the organization. This takes skill, will, and patience. It is a small step for you, and a bigger one for humankind. Color the agreement makers sparkling gold. Spread the word, spread the skill. Perhaps we can eventually admit that our hidden agreement on reality is better than confrontation.

People Problem 4: Pervasive Fear and Threats

Job security is now an oxymoron, a logical inconsistency. Organizations are at the core of our society. These anonymous masses deliver and shape our needs. They are where the jobs are. Getting in, staying in, and prospering has never been easy. But now those three giant stages are totally unpredictable. Even government workers feel the chill of outplacement, replacement, and retrenchment.

In permanent turbulent water, managing fear is the personal skill. Helping others manage theirs is the leadership skill. The level of fear among the management ranks in the United States (those who haven't been let go) has never been higher.

The fear of being outside the protective government shield and over the age of 45 and needing to be engaged in a productive life and to earn a decent living are even higher.

The organizational value-setters misunderstand this fear. To many senior managers it is the sledgehammer needed to pull people into positive appreciation. Just as in the 1930s, "if you can't take the heat, bear the weight, the long line outside has your replacement at the ready." Recycling the threats of foreign competition, sale of the division, and financial gloom and doom does, indeed, keep the fear factor functioning. However, the need is for whatever reassurance can be given, for caring and supportive management attitudes and systems. Implied threats and backroom maneuvering all make it worse. When people are too scared, they get tight, they distort, they exaggerate their self-centeredness, and they eventually undermine the system. Unions understood long ago that to "help improve processes" usually meant that someone would drop through the trap door. The color of fear is black. Fear is an unlikely route to "being in the black" over the long haul, but that doesn't seem to stop many head honchos from using fear in the short run, taking the money and running.

The good news is that the organization of the future will no longer be a maximum security cell! The bad news is that the organization of the future will no longer be a maximum security cell!

People Problem 5: Being Hooked in the Job

The ideal organization has "deeply engaged" people who make it work through whatever difficulties are encountered. The management/leadership crew of the future, however, will be at a level of engagement far beyond the current norm. The trend seems to be toward managers and executives who are mired, embroiled, and round-the-clock "hooked into the job." There is no time out, no time left, no respite, and the tentacles of the job will pull tighter. This state of affairs does not usually bode well for the health of the organization or of the high-energy-expending manager, either. You can have just one job now and be a moonlighter. Or, to put it another way, everyone is now working at least two jobs—his own and the one of the person who got terminated this morning!

Some executives (with wonderfully decadent salaries, bonus plans, and golden parachutes) tell us, "We move the goal line every year. Last year's competence and performance is the old mark. The level of play rises. The comfort zone is free floating. There is little resting, on laurels or on anything else."

One major factor contributing to the trend of hooking managers deeply into their jobs is electronics. If management says, "Stay in touch at all times," we have the means to do it: beepers, cellular phones, computer modems, fax hookups (at home, in the car, at the beach if you can get there), and overnight delivery.

Another contribution to the trend is the global organization. Time zones around the world (where your customers, clients, suppliers, and maybe your boss are located) vary. Europeans are nearing the end of their normal business day as workers in the United States drive to work; in Tokyo, the next day is already beginning as tired commuters head home in the United States. If these are our customers and our competitors, what is a normal work day? When is the manager not, in fact, on duty? Fear lives! Got to hang in there, or you will lose the edge, get the criticism, be seen as a shirker. Keep on trucking. The only thing faster than a fast runner is a scared fast runner!

People Problem 6: Group Work and the Time Bomb

As we mentioned in Chapter 5, one cost of the team-oriented organization is meetings. Teams meet in a seemingly endless parade, discussing issues that were once solved by individuals. Individuals must prepare for all the team meetings and follow up on the meeting assignments.

Team players meet with the team, and the call-backs mount, the E-mail awaits, the customers want attention. If the above mosaic isn't engaging enough, remember that technology, functional skills, management skills, and people skills all need to be updated. Get sharp, stay sharp. The competition (out there), and your competitor (down the hall) are all getting smarter (and working harder, too).

Learning takes time, too. Increasingly, customer service is a "must do," rather than a nicety. If making a late delivery in Denver is your responsibility, you get on it . . . now! Your personal plans are irrelevant; your catching up is secondary.

People Problem 7: The Erosion of the Personal Life

This issue is one of the most murky. The pace is frantic, the needs real, the false starts costly in time. We want people deeply in the game, working hard. When, however, does it become a black hole, a bottomless pit? Smell the roses? Delegate it!

The meaningful life is a balanced one. A career of great achievement can leave an executive deeply disappointed twenty years into it if the rest of his or her life is empty. The executive who demands that people take their vacations, spend time with the family, and take time off to recharge is a laughable rarity. Corporate policy extols its dedication to people. Customer service is also an inside job, it points out with pride. On-stream on a daily basis, however, it is easy to see people as replaceable parts.

Some organizations say frankly that they bring them in young, eager, and energetic. They burn out in two to three years. Next? We cannibalize our people this way. Scrape away the superficialities from these pressures on manager/leaders and color what's left as opportunity. All tools and techniques can be used or abused. There is nothing different here; we're simply using up our people the same way.

People Problem 8: Permanent Expectations and Temporary Realities

A paradox for anyone seeking a long, meaningful life in today's organizations is the knowledge that you are a "temp." Forget the hype when you were hired, the hopes of a 250-year mission for the organization, and the vision painted by the CEO. The new, personal paradigm is one of seeing yourself as temporary. On the grand scale, of course, we are all on temporary assignment anyway (just penciled in). To acknowledge that we are all temps is, in many ways, very freeing.

The future organization will be more flexible and form-fluid as it moves from year to year into new services, products, and markets. Staying nimble and quick is the key. The human resources, then, will consist of some permanent employees, lots of short-term outsiders (the typical "temps"), consultants, and contractors who get the "outsourced" work. And so, as Al Vicere, the associate dean for executive advancement at Penn State, says, you may move through the organization as an employee who is de-hired to a contractor or a consulting basis. You may then become an entrepreneur, be your own consulting organization, and hire others who were recently de-hired by the same company you left. Who is, indeed, on first base today?

As we stated earlier, there is something freeing about this paradigm shift. If you can accept the fact that being a temp is permanent, you are freed of expectations that will be dashed, freed of disappointments. You may also have less reason to be angry, frustrated, or disillusioned. You can put your energies into getting ready, being on-line, being real, and finding ways to use your talents anywhere. There is a movement away from dependency on "the big system." A nice thought. Examine the temp life with your kaleidoscope. Is it getting a job or making a job? If the corporate career is less predictable, can you make your own?

People Problem 9: The Shifting Reward Matrix

Good work used to mean good pay and good advancement. In the flat organization, there is less to aspire to. Middle management shrinks, layers disappear, and each time that happens, hundreds of promotional opportunities disappear—yours, and, of course, everyone else's. How do you get the extreme performance levels the world is demanding from people who have nowhere to go? Organizations will increasingly want to control the salary line. Companies in the United States may even eventually deal with senior executives' excessive total compensation packages.

Routine promotion for good work and the accompanying leap in pay are gone, for you, most likely, and for most of your people. Managing the "poor in prospect" is a skill you may need to acquire. The trick is, of course, to get people to work willingly without that prospect.

People Problem 10: The Stifling of the Artistic, the Poetic, and the Adventurous

Dreaming the desired future, shaping creative responses, and energizing the spirit is done more with the artistic and poetic side of people than with the mildly autistic actuarial side. The nurturing of this side of those who take responsibility adds to their pleasure and the treasure they bring to bear. But this creativity is being stifled by our obsession with numbers, our spartan performance demands, and our "get it done yesterday" mentality.

Creativity requires time, space, money, lack of fear and loose ends—even if only for a couple of days or a couple of decades. Major breakthroughs in products, services, and organizational designs take years of patient nurturing. Just asking for this kind of commitment takes great courage.

Reflections and Refractions

This is a beautifully instructive moment to look back. In the 1980s, we would have listed a very different set of prominent people problems—turnover of good people, poor attendance, union agitation, complaints about appraisals and raises, difficulties in recruiting the best. To some extent, these still exist. However, the recent radical changes in our global marketplace, sociocultural-political alterations, and organizational reconfigurations have brought vastly different problems right inside our workplaces. These new problems have become clearer so recently that there are almost no helpful management theories for dealing with them. Once again, you will have to invent creative responses as you go. Our job at the moment is to tell you that the changes are here, they are real, they will not go away in any short term, and, therefore, they cannot be ignored!

Action Exercise 9–1

Circle the people problems that you think are hindering futurethink and creative questioning in your organization.

1. Functional teams with people from dysfunctional families

2. A world (and organizations) with a bias toward violence

3. The conflict of managing agreement

4. Pervasive fear and threats

5. Being hooked in the job

6. Group work and the time bomb

7. The erosion of the personal life

8. Permanent expectations and temporary realities

9. The shifting reward matrix

10. The stifling of the artistic, the poetic, and the adventurous

What can you do about those you chose?

10

The New Top Ten Problem People

"You're paranoid only if you think they're out to get you and they aren't! Besides, paranoia is just something else to manage!"

Your shipmates on the good ship SS Permanent Turbulent Water have within their hands and hearts the power to make the voyage—and the power to sink the raft with all hands on board. While the angry waters churn and the possibilities surge around you, your attention as leader is often diverted by what are euphemistically called "problem people." Interestingly enough, at one time or another, all of us are problem people, to ourselves and to others. And that's normal.

We believe that nearly all people can and will eventually make a positive contribution. Some employees, of course, should never have been brought on board. Any normal behavior, done to excess, can become a problem. Allowed to spread, certain behaviors become toxic.

Enter yet another paradox. Since people will have new problems to deal with, will there be different kinds of problem people? Or will the unusual employees simply continue the same old behavior patterns that have been passed on through the ages? The answer is the second. Our hunch is that the iterations, the aberrations, and the shapes will be sadly familiar. However, in the millennium, the stakes will be higher, the time frames for responses will be tighter, and the opportunities for problem people to drag down great intentions and derail grand projects will grow exponentially.

You face two possible risks:

1. Problem people can take you out of the game.

2. You may fall into the trap. You could become the problem . . . without having the first clue. If this happens, color yourself an endangered species.

The New Top Ten Problem People

When you examine the crew in your organization, you are likely to find some of these kinds of problem people:

1. *The Teflon Terrorist.* If it ain't broke, break it! If it is broke, fix the blame first! The fixers of blame took Teflon 101 at an early stage and have learned to sprinkle blame and flick off responsibility in any crisis or new venture. They then move quickly to find an available repository. Terrorists, if not challenged, can hold entire departments hostage. They are nurtured and fed by managers who, when confronted with a problem, say "Not me!" and then ask "Who did that?" instead of "What is wrong and how do we make it right?"

Teflon Terrorists prefer a world in which problems are never really solved or fixed. A hopeless, fluid situation always gives them greater room to maneuver. With the stakes higher and the pace quicker, there will be an even higher premium on avoiding blame. The techniques for shifting attention, hiding poor decisions, and covering your tracks will increase.

2. *The Chemically Committed Colleague.* Unfortunately, there is a continuing rise in substance abuse among people who have regular employment—managers, professionals, and just plain doers. Conversationally, depending on the substance of choice,

they're called crackheads, potheads, acidheads, and alcoholics. The use of some exotic substances is rather easy to hide, until job behavior becomes affected. While you are desperately trying to develop a committed workforce, these people meet their needs through agriculture and chemistry. There is increasing speculation that the new world of work is contributing greatly to the need for stress release through chemical routes, both ancient and new.

When and if you become aware of substance abuse in your unit, your first position must be to offer help, seek help, and urge healing and support.

3. *The Electronic Recluse.* Introverts, passive-aggressives, and professional conflict avoiders have been heartened by the advent of electronic mail, telephone answering machines (voice mail), and fax machines. Their objectives are many, not the least of which is to keep on doing what they are doing (or not doing) without any interference. Add the complication of flattened organizations and the resulting direct reporting relationship that resembles a platoon, instead of the traditional knot of six or eight people, and you have entire business cycles completed without face-to-face contact.

In the millennium, high-quality, face-to-face time will become more, not less, important, as a direct result of "people disconnection" caused by growing electronic capabilities. Everyone will avoid dialogue and group meetings as a waste of time and energy. It is in those encounters that the problem people can be confronted and cared for and the focus on reality regained. Bring the recluse back in. Color the electronic recluse "lonely and loving it."

4. *The Power Parasite.* Driven by ego, fear, or perversity, Power Parasites suck in any loose piece of power. Empowerment programs are just their thing. Since any new reshaping of the power relationship surfaces the skepticism and fears of many, these parasites take in all they can. If the Power Parasite is talented, the results, in narrow bands and over short time, can be good. The loss of momentum to the program, however, can be great. Worst of all, any chance of synergy and high-spirited team play is lost. Power Parasites believe that power is an endangered

species and that grabbing what they can before someone else does ensures their safety.

Power Parasites also have a control fetish; no one else can do it as right or as well or as fast. It's my way or the highway. Therefore, they won't share data, insight, or knowledge (information is, indeed, power). They perceive the mentoring of others as similar to career suicide. Power Parasites often fail because the disempowered gleefully let them find the landmines the hard way.

5. *The Supreme Empowerer.* This slickster has developed delegating to an art form. The Supreme Empowerer parcels out and deflects responsibility for any idea to the originator. That way, when people are so overloaded with work that they can't move, the ideas will stop flowing to him. Since everyone else is now doing his job, it's time for golf, or perhaps a tennis match. This slickster is also teflon-coated. He does only what he likes and slides the rest toward the originator of the idea or toward the closest person.

6. *The Frequent Filer.* In every organization of any size, a hard-core group exists that sees personnel-related laws and regulations (e.g., equal opportunity laws, the Americans with Disabilities Act) as ways to manipulate bosses, coworkers, bank accounts, and the system. The Frequent Filer, when unhappy with any turn of events, will whine, pout, cry some form of unfairness, and threaten to file some kind of complaint, grievance, or lawsuit. In hypersensitive, politically correct organizations, such behavior often elicits an instant defensive response and creates a "protective envelope" around the person. From this protected space, the Frequent Filer takes license and sanctimoniously criticizes the "unfair unwashed."

All forms of real discrimination should be dealt with immediately by the manager in charge. But "wolf cries" about things like slightly careless language and minimally controversial decisions should not be resolved in fear of the Frequent Filer. When people increasingly use this legal threat, you will have to get help from your human resources department and hold your ground. Don't reinforce the Frequent Filer!

7. *The Charismatically Challenged CEO.* Boring CEOs can't get or give us what we need. Top dogs often get picked for very

narrow reasons. Specialization in one area often creates "tunnel vision" in other arenas. A CEO can be chosen for his fastball, hook shot, slap shot, headers, or marketing plan. In the age of video, what happens when:

- The CEO is otherwise dull, boring, and uncreative?
- He was the last-place finisher in the charisma contest?
- The CEO's monthly video is used as an antidote for sleeplessness?
- Your exhausted troops are forced to listen to the new, exciting "dream/vision" from this dynamo of dullness, king of clichés, earl of lost enthusiasm, prince of dispassion?

Don't be surprised at the increasing level of snoring and the growing lack of dream acceptance!

8. *The Stimulus Junkie.* Managing Stimulus Junkies in a world requiring increasing concentration is a problem. Stimulus Junkies will proliferate in 2000+. A.D.D. (attention deficit disorder) is synchronized to cultural norms. Enhanced electronic capabilities encourage the short cycle, spastic attention, global boredom, wire-thin patience. No one wants to wait, endure, chill out, or soak. Get up, get moving, get on with it. Stimulus Junkies are problem people and an asset. They are prime candidates for world-class workaholic status when they are able to focus enough to do real work. Organizations speak outwardly with disdain of workaholics, yet encourage them at every turn. Containing and restraining Stimulus Junkies can reduce the associated problems and channel the buzzing energy.

Stimulus Junkies are a real detriment to effective meetings (they contend that all meetings are boring and of no value). They undermine meaningful planning (what's for lunch is their maximum plan-ahead time-frame) and generally exhibit relentless impatience with teammates, bosses, and the organization. Their aura itself can cause dis-ease among associates. Restlessness, irritability, and erratic movements are all tell-tale signs.

Can anything move fast enough, have enough variety and interest to keep them focused? Ponder this question deeply.

9. *The Global Village Idiot.* The electronic and information age has left some people in the dust. Unable and/or unwilling

to get out of her provincial and parochial prison, the Global Village Idiot is so ignorant and out-of-touch that she thinks that the international date line is where the swinging singles go in Fiji; a U.N. mandate is a small tropical fruit; and a megabyte is what you take just before a big gulp!

Global Village Idiots (akin to the V.P. of International Marketing who has no passport), can't enhance their customers' experiences in their own county, let alone the rest of the world.

10. *The Electronic Voyeur.* The manager who overuses and abuses electronic monitoring is a threat to the spirit of the organization. Big brother is watching you. So is little brother, little sister, and the weirdo down the street. The quality of your customer contact may not be argued anymore between boss and employee. It's all in living color, live and on tape. Get the picture? Here's looking at you. This electronic documentation has a great potential for abuse and for preventing abuse for bosses and employees alike! Use it wisely, walk softly, and carry a big on/off switch!

Adding It Up

The solution to these new caricatures hasn't been invented yet, but it begins with identification, awareness, and brain-storming. Some old dogs can be taught new tricks, and it's a marvelous high when you pull it off. Just respect their fears and insecurities—they took time to build and they will take time to tear down! Create your own solid, unique, managerial responses.

Action Exercise 10-1

In your own shop, which types of new problem people are you beginning
to observe, and how often is the behavior occurring?

	Frequency of Observation		
Problem People	Never	Just Surfacing	Often Seen
1. The Teflon Terrorist			
2. The Chemically Committed Colleague			
3. The Electronic Recluse			
4. The Power Parasite			
5. The Supreme Empowerer			
6. The Frequent Filer			
7. The Charismatically Challenged CEO			
8. The Stimulus Junkie			
9. The Global Village Idiot			
10. The Electronic Voyeur			

Action Exercise 10–2

What new problem people do you see just over the horizon?

1.

2.

3.

11

Readying Yourself for a Positive Tomorrow

"Future skills and attitudes: Don't leave home without them: The American Impress Card!"

Just as making laws is too important to trust to lawyers and designing buildings to be inhabited by people is too important to be left to architects and engineers, so, too, your personal development plan is too vital to leave to someone else, a basically uninterested third party—the organization.

Just as the field of succession planning and management development began to mature, it became irrelevant. Elaborate plans to shape the skills and insights of managers and professionals became meaningless in the downsizing, outsourcing, and reconfiguration of the organization. Focusing on "moving up" in a system with fewer middle management positions means preparing for a war never to be fought. Participants in the big divisional annual development program barely get invested in the process, knowing they will be "windowed out" (early retirement enticement) in the next round of "right-sizing." If your organization does, in fact, offer training and development, take it on; just be sure it fits in with a broad, well-rounded personal development program that you have shaped and sorted out.

Preparing for a Positive Future

Few would argue that being positive about yourself, your organization, and your world is good for you. How does one achieve that in the face of what seems to be permanent calamity on the trip through permanent white water? It happens by changing your expectations and your self-view and then getting ready. For example, if you hang onto the old expectations (still proclaimed by most organizations), you may be left hanging.

The view of the organization's responsibility to the employee has been radically altered. An interesting thing happened on the way to changing the contract among employees, employees with some promise (those on the "management track"), and the organization. The potential contract items are the same, but the emphasis has changed.

Old Contract

- Security
- A career of advancement and promotion for the skilled and the loyal and/or the sacrificial.

New Contract

- A place to make a difference, a genuine contribution
- Opportunity to experience personal growth and learning

There is a lot of evidence that organizations not only don't want to provide pockets of security or elaborate tracks for advancement; they no longer have the power! It's gone. It's out of reach. Even government agencies are being pushed to do more with less and to reinvent themselves.

Therefore, the individual has a duty to herself to pursue the outcome items in the contract that are now the currency of the future—making a difference and using the organization as a mechanism for personal learning. These new expectations require a new level of readiness and an unfolding personal development.

The Vision of People of Promise

- Take the long view and seek the big picture.
- Become valuable wherever you are.
- Become fully inserted in unfolding events.
- Be ready to move on, move out, move into new happenings.
- Be alive and well when outside the system so that you go on with fulfilling the promise.
- Learn, grow, and change every step of the way.
- Be open to all that is happening.
- Develop a wide range of behaviors.
- Be emotionally grounded and rounded.
- Connect to others in ways that support and enhance high, focused energy.
- Develop an attitude that handles the good and the bad in a positive way.

The Positive Perspective

Take a reading on your energy level. Is it positive, negative, neutral (and proud of it), or, perhaps, desperately destructive or depressed? To take a reading, check out some of these things.

Listen to your inner dialogue and the music. If you stopped almost anyone, at any time, and asked what she was doing at that moment, and she was aware, she would say, "I am talking to myself." What is going on in that dialogue with yourself? Is it filled with "atta girls" and "atta boys," or is it a litany of put-downs and self-dumpings? "Down dummy!" or "Way to go, klutz!" or "Spastic man roars again!" Your inner dialogue is a choice of your own in a script of your making. Much of it was learned as you grew up, and some you picked up because your peer group banged on people with negative drivel. You can expunge most of that over time. On the other hand, until you can fine-tune the right stuff, notice what's playing at the little theater in your head even if you can't notice the impact. We tend, as we have said before, to perform that which we envision. If the descriptive narrative inside the brain is a barrage of "Way to go, dingbat!," it will be hard to channel much in a positive way. Clues to the messages come sometimes by the music and the words to the music. What's playing in your head? Is it upbeat, happy, or is it dreary stuff?

Your positive energy index is measured, too, by the destructive behaviors you keep doing, such as:

- Drinking to still the noises in your head
- Driving when you are angry or stoned
- Smoking heavily
- Skipping the seat belt
- Arguing in parking lots about a space (getting in the face of strangers)

Doing one or several of these things is usually a sign of self-disrespect and disregard. Plain old interpersonal feedback will also expand your energy index accuracy. Ask someone who is reasonably positive, grounded, and sensitive to people about your positivity ratio. If it is less than you would like, listen to your justifications—"Well, you would, too, if you had a boss like mine." And so forth. Of course, other people sift your actions and feelings through their own headsets. Such views are truly other people's views and are tainted by their biases.

Next, get the unvarnished picture. Set up an audiotape as you talk in your office or sit in a meeting. Ask to have the next staff meeting videotaped. Everyone will get an astonishing picture of who is listening, zapping, supporting, and spacing out. You will be there, too. Take a look at the film. It is your "attitude appraisal," if not your performance appraisal.

Detoxify Your System

If you have been smiling warmly through much of the preceding section, you most likely have found the positive perspective. You live it, love it, and wish it on others. You already know that detoxing your environment is both an internal and an external job. Here are some ways to accomplish it:

- Stop zapping others. Stop discounting and putting them down.
- Stop using sarcasm and making snide remarks even though you think they are great fun.
- Stop aiming for a black belt in mouth karate. Mouth attacks provide a few good laughs, but they are cheap because they come at another person's expense. The real cost, though, is the energy that everyone in the nickel-rocket network expends protecting himself and loading up for the next assault. If someone is always loaded to dump on you, that person has invested some time and energy to resurface the attack. The preparation for this dumping game represents time and energy that is lost to the organization and pulls our focus away from the real things we want to accomplish.

As a community player (at home, in the neighborhood, or in the career setting), stop the cynics everywhere. Resign from the games, and call them on their behaviors. Be prepared—cynics are subtle. They may respond with "Why are you upset? I was just kidding. It's all good clean fun." The drivers of this behavior are ideas such as:

- No good deed will go unpunished here.
- Excuse me, you must have mistaken me for someone who cares.
- If this turns out well, we may get the blame.
- We'll burn that bridge when we come to it.

It is no big deal to step out of the game of "zap." And it is refreshing sometimes to invite people to stop picking on each other. Picking on people uses negative energy, and the hostility in these words is just beneath the surface. Change the people you spend your time with. Find the optimistic, the positive, the can-do people, and be there with them and for them.

Clearing the Channels for Positive Energy

The quality of energy you have available to offer your organization or yourself depends on unclogging your system, emptying your bucket, and clearing your channels. Here are some simple steps to help do this:

1. Let go of that which you did not get—the opportunity that evaded you and the window that closed before you got there.

2. Check your bitterness index, your disappointment scale, and your general hostility level. Again, you can ask others, and if it seems as if you really want to know, they may even tell you. On the other hand, you already know, don't you?

To detox, letting go of the negative stuff is all in the readiness package. Misery is optional. Remember that bad things happen to all of us, and you have a choice of how they will affect you. "You make me mad" is just another disempowering statement. The truth is that someone did something you didn't like or didn't want. You could get mad, get bored, laugh, fall down, or take a nap. Getting mad was *your* choice!

Forgiveness is a virtue our society handles poorly. As Jerry Harvey said in the "Abilene Paradox," it is the source of blame fixing: Since I can't take the blame without being beaten about it, I do a coverup and distance myself from the event.[1] Forgiveness is a virtual roto-rooter for clearing your personal channels. Don't tell the negative others, though. They probably can't handle forgiveness and will see it as another ploy. Just do it. Be freed to move on. Like we say, "Next?".

An essential step in "going positive" is owning the negative. Sitting on anger only builds it up. Anger will eat at you and end up in one or more of the many sidebars that anger creates: stomach ulcers, sour dispositions, serious illnesses, depression. People who "introvert" their anger suffer physiological

---

1. Jerry B. Harvey, "The Abilene Paradox: The Management of Agreement," *Organizational Dynamics* 3, no. 1 (Summer 1974): 63–80.

and/or emotional crises over time. Other people externalize it. They sit on their anger until it builds up, boils over, and splatters on everyone in a destructive scene. It feels good for a while, but there are also other consequences. Clearing your channel of anger is a long learning process for those who have suffered the pains. It can be done by acquiring skills in confronting the need directly and improving your problem-solving capabilities.

Increasing the Positive

Becoming positive, we suspect, is a growing thing. It has to be wanted and pursued. Try these two steps.

1. *Listen for the wake-up call.* The anger and fear that you feel may simply be a cover for a deeper discontent with the way you are living out your life or career. It may be an internal buzz, an itch, a feeling or dis-ease. The buzz of activity works well to drown out the sounds, thoughts, and feelings.

2. *Write a personal vision.* Begin the process now. Write down five things you want to like about yourself. State those likes in "here and now" terms, such as "I am engaged with others in successful undertakings." Your personal vision can contain anything you want: you and your job, the shape of a career, the personal attitudes and emotional changes you want, the relationships you want. Spell them out. Be specific. Describe yourself as the person you want to spend the rest of your life with. Sprinkle it with accomplishment, fun, and exploration. Update it often. Pull it out, refer to it, aspire to it, change it when needed.

Changing the Inner Dialogue

Sound too simple? Maybe, maybe not. Just begin by saying good things to yourself about yourself. If you have made a few stabs at your vision, quote from that. Read it to yourself. Some people call these affirmations. Others refer to them as positive self-programming. They may help a lot. They will never hurt you. Here are some examples:

- I am positive and open to possibilities.
- I am always in the right place at the right time doing the right things.
- I am unique and unfolding.
- I build strong positive relationships in my professional role and throughout all my life.
- I handle change readily and learn good things each time.
- I enjoy my job and reflect that to others around me.

The vision, the affirmations, and the urge to focus a powerful positive energy are often found on the quiet side. Any of the solitary, private practices (prayer, silent reflection, meditation) can help. The answers, the integration of events and options, the explanations and understandings happen in the unexpected.

There is a "half-tone" that taps into the subconscious that anyone can achieve. It is as simple as repeating a sound over and over to yourself or permitting your eyes to defocus while you are quiet. The answers may be vividly there for you or may emerge at a later, unexpected time while you are driving, taking a shower, or falling asleep.

Grounding and centering skills can be taught! For example, Tai' Chi and other martial arts can help some people open up their energy channels in an effective way. Needless to say, this evades the Stimulus Junkie and professional fibrillator, hard-charging through day after day. Insights aren't often found while you're running at full, oxygen-gasping speed.

Positive Paranoia

The Positive Paranoid believes that out there somewhere, anywhere, someone is waiting to do her a lot of good. However, the Positive Paranoid has to overcome cultural programming. Action Exercise 11–1 lists statements with a blank space. Typically programmed cultural responses are basically negative. Try them on for size.

Outrageous Optimism

As you magnify your positive valence, you may want to demonstrate dramatic positivity. You may want to be outrageously positive, the seeker of many ponies in awful situations. You may want to be the one who takes the positive stand, who accepts the challenge. People of promise are not defined by quarterly reports, stock prices, and the annual performance appraisal. They care, but in a focused way that encourages people, including themselves, to make a difference by being different. In some organizations, that alone makes them outrageous. Attitude and emotional evolution are the ultimate learning for people of promise.

The Contradictions Continue

No one is going to coddle you. We are team collaborators, and we help each other. You are only young once, but you can be immature forever. You enrich your contribution by being childlike, not childish. You move toward the positive as you express the negative. Often, the more negative the situation, the more you can learn about positivity.

Negative Energy Is Better Than No Energy

As leaders of management group training sessions, we often have to deal with a negative audience. The participants may be filled with anger, hostility, and resentment at having to be there. This crowd walks in with an "attitude" and is negatively energized. Angry groups are far better groups to train than apathetic audiences. At least the energy (albeit negative) is already up and running. All we have to do is humorously point out that we are aware of their plight and it's okay and then reprogram the cannon and aim it in another direction. The charge is already lit. Apathetic groups must do much more work to make progress. Getting them to care is tougher than redirecting the negative enthusiasm.

Improving Organizations Through Energy

Most organizations aren't well but are working on it. They need a flood of positive energy, and the best source of affirmative ingredients are the people of promise. In the end, the outcomes for people of promise are simple and dramatic:

- Become a culture shaper.
- Be a solution maker.
- Be a part of the long view.
- Be in the act of becoming, in the act of doing.

The Organizational Dream/Vision/Mission/ Values Thing

If you haven't seen it, heard it, been asked about it, or been dumped on with it—the mission/vision/values thing is the core of organization theory about itself. As we explained in Chapter 4, the need for dreams and direction is real. But the "acting out" of the dream is often just another sham, a fruitless exercise or an annual training objective. Direction setting is the core of the leadership job. Where are we going? How will we get there? To what purpose? Sailing according to what values vector? If the dream/vision/mission/values thing comes your way, we suggest that you learn the technology and the theory and struggle with your mates to add your insights and hopes to the definition process. If it fails, you have learned something, anyhow.

There is, however, no reason to be cynical or bitter. A master craftsman doesn't blame his tools! All tools can be used in positive or punishing and destructive ways. The direction-setting tools are no different.

Your Personal Dream/Vision/Mission/ Values Thing

The discussion of direction setting is very powerful on a personal level, but who has the time these days, right? If you don't have a destination or outcome solidly in mind, why should any-one else care if you don't get it done? If you aren't aware and clear about the life quality and exhilarating side trips you could and should achieve, they probably won't happen. So just do it! Sit down, dream a while (six days or six months is okay), and write it down as it flows. Tell other people about your process and the stage of your dreams. Understand the deeper theory about dream making that says that, as you spend quality time pondering what you want to do and be when you grow up, the ideas and forms will begin to come into focus, to flow, emerge, "conflute" (as in confluence) when they are ready. This is not an act of "loneliness" but an "alone-ness" endeavor. It is not (sorry about that) a left-brain, mechanical, drive-it-through experience. You have to start by believing that this "getting in touch with your own aspirations" process is important and will make a dif-ference. You don't run away; you find something exciting to run toward.

Another way to perceive this personal journey is that the "quest," the seeking of your preferred destination, is actually the most important part. To stop the treadmill and to take a de-liberate role in how you do things and what that achieves for you may be the biggest payoff of all. Getting there (athletes often say) is what it's about. But enough of this process theory—the believing that the fun is, indeed, in the going and in the en-ergy in that trip that makes it all happen. Make the commit-ment! Create the event right here and now! At least, think about it?

Discovering Your Values Base

To begin, decide what you stand for, what you aspire to be or have, what you can't live without. What would make your life full and whole? What do you cherish? What is your "vital few," the essentials for you? Be specific; spell them out. If you can't seem to dredge up something, think of the three most successful experiences in your life to this point. What made them success-ful in your eyes? What makes you happy? What are you passion-ate about?

As the next step (and/or if you are stumped at this point), ask someone who knows you (and cares about you) to offer some candid observations about when that person perceives that you are happy, excited, or peaceful. Make a list.

Start here and now:

- I believe in . . .
- I want to be a part of . . .
- I am most alive when I . . .
- I love to . . .
- I get excited about . . .
- I am most at peace when . . .
- I would like to accomplish . . .
- I would most like to be known for . . .

Write your answers to these items on a blank sheet of paper and date your comments. Just starting and overcoming inertia is a huge step. Next, set the list aside, and come back to it in a week or two. Now that you have begun to think about your dream, you need to let the thoughts incubate. Over the next few days, as your mind occasionally wanders over what you wrote, new ideas, new connections, revisions, and rejections of your first ideas will come, often at the oddest times. When we have begun a project, we get some of our best ideas when exercising, shaving, driving (keep a note pad with you at all times), and having dinner.

Values are deep and abiding, and if you have become jaded and cynical, it will take a while for them to surface or resurface. By the way, you may have changed since you last even thought about your life. Be patient. Be kind to yourself (one of our values). Please try it—honestly and earnestly. Let's see what happens.

Your Mission

If organizations can have (and should have) mission statements, so can you. Even the basic organizational theory fits:

- Who are you?
- What do you want to be or do?

- Who are your clients? (Force yourself to put them in order of importance; prioritizing them is critical to making any decision, because they compete for your time and energy.)
- What need(s) do you fulfill? (What were you put on this earth to be or do?)
- How do you make that happen?

There is one more question, one that we have saved for last. Without answering it, you will not achieve as much. The question is, How will I know when I have done what I intended? What are the outcomes that will define the successful completion of my current mission?

Deciding who you want to be and what you want to do is your job! Defining success is a personal task. Individual dreams, vision, missions, and values are do-it-yourself toolkits! This is one job that you can't delegate to others! No one else has your thoughts, feelings, loves, and aspirations. Success is whatever you decide it is! But do get started—do think about it—do decide!

Adding It Up

Right, wrong, but never indifferent, we have tried to get you to see some things just over the horizon. We have provided the obvious and not-so-obvious indicators that we believe are important to getting in, staying in, and stepping out of organizations when you want. We encourage you always to examine new ways and to decide for yourself whether the changes are meaningful or faddish.

We have tried to update you on the strategies and use of dreams, teams, motivation, and schemes. These skills are relatively enduring but need fine-tuning as the world around you changes.

Finally, we have tried to provide our best advice on the strategies that will help you not only to survive but to live a meaningful, bountiful, useful life. Your survival and success are in your hands (but that's where they've always been). Right?

Reading any book is like shopping for clothes at the mall. Many new garments just aren't your style. If something catches your eye, try it on. If it doesn't fit, don't buy it or get it tailored to meet your needs. But if you like the color, style, price, and fit—take it home!

The prevailing managers of tomorrow will have *Faith, Hope,* and *Clarity!*

Action Exercise 11-1

Take a few minutes and fill in the blanks below. How do most people view things?

Thank God it's _____!

The world is out to do me _____.

_____ understands me!

Some mornings when I get up I want to call in _____!

I harbor _____ feelings about life.

People often _____-mouth their own organization.

The boss likes to catch people doing things _____.

You have to learn to take the good with the _____.

Why does everything _____ always happen to me?

Gawd, ain't it _____?

If you want a quick answer, it's _____.

If you smile too much here, people will think you are _____.

If you are calm in the midst of chaos, people will _____.

If you want it done right, then _____.

You _____ have to be crazy to work here.

Action Exercise 11-2
(Positive Paranoia)

The positive employee might respond in the following ways.

Thank God it's *Monday!*

The world is out to do me *good!*

Everyone understands me (if I explain myself)!

Some mornings when I get up I want to call in *well!*

I harbor *good* feelings about life.

People often *good*-mouth their own organization.

The boss likes to catch people doing things *right.*

You have to learn to take the good with the *wonderful.*

Why does everything *great* always happen to me?

Gawd, ain't it *wonderful?*

If you want a quick answer, it's *yes!*

If you smile too much here, people will think *you are really happy!*

If you are calm in the midst of chaos, people will see you as *a source of strength!*

If you want it done right, then *teach people how to do it right!*

You *don't* have to be crazy to work here.

Action Exercise 11-3
Personal Dream/Vision/Mission/Values Statement

My dream/vision is to:

_____

_____

_____

My mission in life is to: _____

_____

_____

_____

The things I treasure (value) the most are:

1.

2.

3.

4.

5.

Action Exercise 11-4

As someone once said, we have all drunk from wells we did not dig and been warmed by fires we did not build. Dream! Hope! See yourself there! When we work with leaders of organizations, we often ask these questions. They are the starting point for understanding a leader and her vision. The questions, however, are grounded, in a very personal sense.

1. When you look back on your career some years down the road, what legacy do you want to leave in place?

2. What will those you lead and those who lead with you say was your greatest contribution to the organization?

3. What will you want to leave in place (a process, a program, a vision, a set of values, a competitive positioning) that will be the foundation of a long, successful future?

4. What will others have noticed about what you learned? Your resilience? Your growth as a person as you handled your career?

Action Exercise 11-5

Aerobics is more than just a physical activity. Develop a broad set of management exercises in your organizational life that will give you increased stamina, resilience, strength, and confidence.

Read the environment. Scope out the surrounding components, trends, opportunities, threats, actions, results, tone, and relevance. Some major nooks and crannies to scope out include:

1. What business are we really in?

2. What is the main business problem here? How are we responding to it?

3. What is the "state of the organization" right now?

4. What are the trends in our industry or our role with customers?

5. What is our vision/mission, and is it vibrant, visible, and venerable or vague, vacant, and vexing? (Is it worthwhile, alive, and up-front or boring, ignored, and gathering dust?)

6. If you were king or queen for a day, what change would you make right now to improve the way things are?

7. Who is making a great contribution right now and needs to hear more appreciation for that good work from me? From others?

8. Who are the major sources of poor work, the initiators of foul play, and the creators of fogs of negativity? Who cares about that enough actually to do something?

9. What is working so well right now that it should be spread around to others and built upon?

10. What did we promise to do "way back when" that we have let slide? How do we recapture our credibility by getting that moving now?

11. What assumptions do we need to check out for validity? Are they changing? Did we notice?

Action Exercise 11-6

Everything is not as it first seems. Exercise your mind regularly to become more proficient at reading between the lines and checking further possibilities. Practice asking more penetrating questions, such as:

1. How exactly does that affect us?

2. What are we really trying to do here?

3. What are the hidden costs?

4. Why is that important now?

5. What is causing that?

Action Exercise 11-7

To be a permanent temp and an organizational nomad getting ready for the next unknown assignment, you must learn to manage your own personal learning. Start with a change in perspective:

1. What is the one thing you would do if we could guarantee you that you couldn't fail?

2. List three purely selfish things that you would want to do for yourself if there were no consequences.

3. What nontangible gift would you give to yourself?

4. What would you most like to change about your job and career?

5. What do you need to learn to be more effective in your job and organization?

6. What do you need to learn about the career field or profession you are in or about an emerging, new, related field?

7. What personal learnings will be important to you in the next five years? (These can be about work, sports, relationships, communications, or deeper matters of the spirit and personal energy.)

Action Exercise 11-8

Think about what we have tried to convey in this book. Choose three ideas that you want to try out.

Idea 1:

Idea 2:

Idea 3:

Epilogue:
The Millennium Manager's
Bill of Rights

Managers as a group have had very few rights, and what rights they did have seem to be gone for good. Managers formerly had power, privileges, and great possibilities. They never had protection against favoritism and arbitrary treatment. It was survival of the "fit." Your hiring date was your only security clause. The bad news is that our society has done a good job of protecting the rights of consumers, hourly workers, and even criminals, whereas managers have little recourse against injustice and are often left to hang and swing in the breeze.

The good news is that a few new organizations have adopted a more humane and respectful culture. The bad news is that the reason fewer managers are being abused is that there are fewer managers. Corporate downsizings have reduced the management ranks considerably. Nowadays managers are expected to work harder and longer and to be grateful they are still employed. Change can bring new justifications for old tendencies.

This epilogue is a small beginning, but we want to propose a Bill of Rights for Managers. Surely, in the next century these principles won't be too much to ask.

Rights

Right 1:   AS A MANAGER, I HAVE THE RIGHT to be one of a kind, to feel good about myself as I am and can become, to be responsible for living my own life, to know what I know, feel what I feel, speak for myself, and seek what is best for me. When the organization wants to help me grow, help me along, or help me up, I am my own best expert. Help is defined by the helpee. In this way, I bring more to the table, at work, at home, or anywhere else.

Right 2:   AS A MANAGER, I HAVE THE RIGHT to a visible, competent, accessible leader. In this way I can be more effective, efficient, and successful. I shouldn't be expected to waste my time in an organization that is badly managed.

Right 3:   AS A MANAGER, I HAVE THE RIGHT to a worthy vision, clear and consistent goals, reasonably fair rewards, and the resources needed for meeting these targets. These allow me to be motivated and committed to the work, the organization, and my colleagues.

Right 4:   AS A MANAGER, I HAVE THE RIGHT to full disclosure about my organization, my job, and what it takes to "make it" here. Management by mind-reading is an inaccurate, destructive, and narrowly dispensed skill.

Right 5:   AS A MANAGER, I HAVE THE RIGHT to a job in an ethical organization attempting to enrich the lives of those it serves inside and outside of the organization. The more socially conscious the organization is, the better.

Right 6:   AS A MANAGER, I HAVE THE RIGHT to learn, grow, and develop personally and professionally toward my own definition of success. This freedom and growth enhance my motivation and loyalty to the organization.

Right 7:   AS A MANAGER, I HAVE THE RIGHT to a totally private self, a personal life, and the time to pursue that. Workaholics set bad examples in most arenas of life and rarely can sustain long, healthy careers. They infect the organization with dis-ease!

Right 8:   AS A MANAGER, I HAVE THE RIGHT to develop my own management style on the basis of my unique abilities and personality.

Right 9:   AS A MANAGER, I HAVE THE RIGHT (at times) to inclusion or exclusion regarding collaboration, cooperation, teamwork, and empowerment. "No" is the most empowering (and dangerous) word in any organization. At some reasonable point, I have the right to say no to misplaced obsessions.

Right 10: AS A MANAGER, I HAVE THE RIGHT to reject craziness in organizational leadership. I have the right to see through synthetic slogans, quick fixes, and phony programs and projects that deflect instead of focusing energy on real issues.

Right 11: AS A MANAGER, I HAVE THE RIGHT to an honest, caring, fair, playful, and supportive environment where feedback is regular and positively constructive. Direct, daily talk about the core of the job beats performance appraisal interviews, hands down!

Right 12: AS A MANAGER, I HAVE THE RIGHT to personal contact with people while I work. Electronic devices are not sufficient and can create group isolation.

Responsibilities

In exchange for these rights, I have the following responsibilities:

- To give my best effort, best creativity, and best intentions every day
- To be as productive as I can be in my job
- To stay current and dedicated to my profession
- To be positive and speak positively about my organization
- To be loyal to my organization and the colleagues who journey with me

The time of teams and inclusion are upon us in a global economy. The employment contract has changed, too, making long-term stays in organizations less often the reality we will live. Therefore, well-developed, strong, centered, and capable individual managers who can deftly move among projects, groups, and organizations are critical to our global future. These rights and responsibilities embody an open exchange whose time has come!

These rights are essential as we disassemble organizations as we knew them.

Index